CW01671727

£2.25
net

GOOD HOUSEKEEPING
FAMILY LIBRARY

FLOWER ARRANGING

& HOUSE-PLANTS

Titles in the
Good Housekeeping Family Library
include:

Doing Up Your Home
Family Cookery
Family Health
Gardening
Home Medical Handbook
Jams and Preserves
Needlework for Pleasure

GOOD HOUSEKEEPING
FAMILY LIBRARY

FLOWER ARRANGING

& HOUSE-PLANTS

Violet Stevenson

Ebury Press, London

First published 1973 by
Ebury Press
Chestergate House, Vauxhall Bridge Road,
London SW1V 1HF

ISBN 0 85223 033 8

Except where otherwise credited,
all pictures, including cover, by
Leslie Johns.

Filmsetting in Britain by
Typesetting Services Ltd, Glasgow.
Printed and bound in Belgium by
Henri Proost & Cie p.v.b.a., Turnhout

CONTENTS

	Foreword	7
1	A Philosophy of Flower Arranging	9
2	Principles of Design	14
3	Choosing your Container	38
4	Preparation and Equipment	45
5	Long-Lasting Arrangements	53
6	Flowers for Special Occasions	64
7	The Flower Arranger's Garden	82
8	Flowers You Buy	93
9	Happy House-Plants	107
10	Bulbs through the Year	135
11	ABC of Rewarding Indoor Plants	143
	Index	157

FOREWORD

Flower arranging in the west, like needlework and cookery, tends to be associated with femininity. But whereas no woman expects to be able to crochet a bedspread or make puff pastry without learning how to, many seem to feel that they ought to know by instinct, simply by virtue of their sex, how to arrange a bowl of daffodils gracefully. Yet for every woman who prides herself on being 'good with flowers', there are many more who lack this confidence. This is surely one of the reasons for the enormous popularity of flower arranging clubs and classes throughout the country.

There are other and more positive reasons, as Violet Stevenson—a pioneer in this field whose writings and lectures have contributed so much to the current interest in the subject—conveys in this book. Anyone who takes a little trouble to learn how to arrange flowers will find that she has embarked on a pastime which is at the same time stimulating and relaxing, an interest which will grow as the seasons change and which can last a lifetime. On a strictly practical level, she will also find that she gets far greater rewards from her flowers. 'Flower arrangement is really all about getting value', says the author, 'value for flowers you grow and flowers you buy. If you cannot see them all properly and see them at their best, you are simply not getting value'.

Violet Stevenson lives in the country surrounded by over 100 plants which she loves dearly but unsentimentally. 'Remember that humans must come before plants', she says and warns against letting your *Hedera helix* encroach on the ceiling, or your *Monstera deliciosa* spread over the window. If your problem is the reverse—ailing plants that fail to thrive whatever you do to them—she offers much useful advice to help you succeed with your indoor gardening.

Isabel Sutherland
General Editor
Good Housekeeping Family Library

1 A PHILOSOPHY OF FLOWER ARRANGING

For most people, the purpose of flower arranging is to decorate the home; there are some who are also interested in exhibiting at flower shows, but the second pastime is really an extension of the first and essentially, flower arrangement is one of the domestic arts. But this does not mean that it should be regarded as a chore. Although it is a simple art form, it can help to stretch the imagination, crystallise one's thoughts and ideas on many things other than flowers, teach one to use one's hands, to furnish a home with an individual and distinctive touch and to learn about plants and gardening. It also provides an opportunity to express, even to discover, one's personality and individuality.

Flower arrangement really can teach you to see with new eyes; you learn that it is not only the flowers of a plant which are beautiful and decorative and that there are many other materials waiting to be appreciated and used. And the appealing thing about this art is that the materials can be as common and easy to find as the handful of dandelion clocks on page 20, or as choice and exotic as the trio of orchids on page 104.

What's in a flower? Anything that grows or once grew on a plant is a flower in the arranger's sense of the word. As the eye becomes trained and grows keener and more selective and appreciative, the arranger notices things which had previously escaped attention, and graduates from using a bunch of bought flowers on their own to furnish a vase to employing a wide range of materials more subtle in their appeal. Often these are also of a longer lasting quality and of greater decorative worth in their surroundings.

In modern arrangements we like to harmonise not only colours but also forms and textures. This means that we accept the use of all types of plant materials. In the same way that there is no limit to these beyond their suitability to the occasion, so there is no limitation to the kind of vessels in which they may be placed. Once again, the only criterion is that these also should be suited to their setting, and of course that they should be water-tight. Not all the most popular of today's 'vases' were originally meant for flowers, which is probably why arrangers prefer to call them 'containers'. If you look at the arrangements illustrated in this book, you will see that the vessels used range from a tea caddy to a copper saucepan.

Professionals and amateurs

There is no *correct* style of flower arrangement. Each country, or sometimes even part of a country, tends to have a predominant style which could be called national. It is one which the expert can quickly recognise as having been assembled or created by, say, a Dutchman, German, American or Malayan. However, there are certain designs or patterns which can be recognised as being universal.

For example, one would not expect to see much difference (except in materials) in a bowl of flowers designed for the centre of a table in any country where one sits down to dine. In the same way flowers designed for very special or even state occasions also tend to be much alike. This is due partly to the universality of the professional florist, who today is bound to his foreign colleagues by world-wide associations, who benefits by the circulation of new ideas and methods and who is even expected to work to international pattern guides to produce a standard product at an internationally agreed price.

However, flower arrangement is by no means confined to the professional. Tens of thousands of amateurs indulge in this pleasant art form. Evening classes in flower arrangement are extremely popular as are flower arrangement clubs and societies; many of these have members who are qualified and willing to travel and lecture. This means that the influence of the amateur is greater than that of the professional and so we find that there are many styles of arrangement as well as many kinds of materials used in those arrangements that are of no importance commercially.

Usually the difference between professional flower arrangements and also between the national styles of arrangement lies in the kinds of flowers favoured. Any style adopted by any flower arranger inevitably follows the supply of materials available. Thus in urban areas where flowers have to be bought and may be costly, or in countries where during a lengthy period of the year only a few flowers are available, the accent tends to be on making a few flowers go a long way. Accessories and settings take on greater importance under such circumstances.

The western posy

In the western world we have always had plenty of flowers and foliage at hand at most times of the year and it is not unimportant that due to our climate these are long-lasting. Consequently we have not adopted the philosophic and sophisticated attitude towards their arrangement that is found in the ancient school of Japanese arrangement. Our decorators take their time over arranging the flowers, but for different reasons from those of the ancient Japanese masters. Time is spent in massing many flowers rather than in the contemplation of three or a few more. Western styles are seldom frugal.

Our table centre bowl of flowers is a legacy from the tied, tight posy of many mixed flowers, often collared with fern, often wild, sometimes herbal and considered prophylactic, which were once sold in great numbers in the local markets or gathered from gardens to sweeten the air at home. And today, even though the flowers are now arranged individually, we tend still to follow the traditional posy patterns when we display them. Our own national styles, and those of our near neighbours, are generally variations on this posy theme.

Fusion of east and west

Western arrangements tend to be fulsome and colourful. In the east, on the other hand, and for many reasons—economic, climatic and traditional—fewer flowers are used. These are invariably arranged so that they fall within the outline of an irregular triangle. Rules are much stricter.

But like all other arts, flower arrangement is fluid and ever-changing, and so we have many facets of these two basic themes. One important fusing of the two styles can be seen very frequently in American arrangements, where they are joined to create an exciting and practical contemporary style which is virtually an amalgam of line and mass.

Just as the east has influenced our style of flower arrangement, so is the west gradually influencing the beautiful but frugal patterns of the east. Universally, the term 'flower' arrangement is more comprehensive than might at first appear. We use the part for the whole. In all countries today the term 'flower' covers any type of plant materials, and paradoxical though it may appear, many arrangements contain no true flower in the botanical sense. Obviously leaves and branches, grasses, blossom and berries form a part of many flower arrangements, as one would expect, since these materials have been accepted for so long, but less obviously, perhaps, so do all sorts of other materials such as roots, fungi, lichens, driftwood, seed heads, plant embryos and skeletons and even seaweeds.

Finding the right container

People who favour oriental-styled arrangements tend to search for containers that have an oriental appearance (even though these may actually be of modern western ceramics) for it is important, if the completed arrangement is to be harmonious in every way, that the container and the flowers suit each other. This applies to any style of arrangement, not just the Japanese. Since so many more kinds of 'flowers' are acceptable it is only natural that the vessels to hold them should also be chosen with imagination and sensitivity and that these should vary considerably according to the taste, the possessions or even the income of the arranger.

For centuries flower vases have tended to be things apart, their role instantly recognisable, vessels designed and made only to support and display flowers. 'To do the flowers' really does mean something slightly different from 'to make a flower arrangement' and this is true of all countries. Those who 'do' the flowers tend to use only true flowers and flower vases. But for the imaginative and creative flower arranger anything can be used so long as it can be made to hold water or some water-retentive material. It follows that the same container must suit the flowers, their setting and the occasion for which they are being used.

'Period' arrangements

This is not to say by any means that modern flower arrangers eschew true vases. Most people have a collection of many types of vases and containers. Some feel that it is not right to place a very modern flower arrangement in a room full only of antique furniture, particularly if this be of only one period. It is certainly possible to arrange the flowers to suit the room. Period flower ensembles can be made in the style known to be fashionable at the time in question and stood in vessels made or used during the same period. A study of contemporary books and illustrations will usually provide a guide. Often faithful reproductions can be used, or even genuine antiques themselves, protected, if necessary, against damage. In fact, unless originals or copies of originals are used it is sometimes difficult to capture the true flavour of the period. And to be precise, arrangements ought to contain flowers grown and known at the same time rather than obviously modern hybrids.

On the other hand, it should be possible for someone who has studied flower arrangement to make an apt and beautiful arrangement by mingling and mixing plant materials, textures, colours and container so that it suits the surrounding furnishings, even though they be products of another age. Modern flower arrangements need not be strident anachronisms.

Solutions for 'problem' settings: If in doubt, you can always play safe with arrangements made only from the soft hues of foliage. The burnished leaves of young maple, the summer green and the autumnal-tinted leaves of beech, soft grasses and ageless ferns will not dominate lovely pieces of furniture or ornaments, nor will the gentle sheen of the leaves vie with centuries-old polish and patina.

Often it is best to focus attention upon the container and let its contents play a subordinate role, melting into the background like a piece of faded embroidery or mellow porcelain. Old pewter, copper and brass not only suit flowers in texture but because they are metals actually help the flowers to last longer. Wooden containers, especially those of mahogany (such as old tea caddies) look well with simple flowers, old roses, wallflowers, pansies and wild flowers for example, all of which are quite delightful. Because they do not belong to any specific age such containers are at home in any setting.

Sometimes a still life assembled in the manner of a Dutch flower painting will suit a 'problem' setting best. This often can be made from a mixture of dried and fresh flowers and so will not demand constant attention.

Those who have homes in which there are furniture and furnishings of different periods will find that the right kind of flower arrangements, strategically placed, will link one to the other in a pleasant and unobtrusive manner. Others with modern homes will learn that for them the content and styles of flower arrangement are limitless. They can experiment, improvise, originate, blend and create even if only a few kinds of flowers are available to them.

Using plants in decoration

The role of potted plants in decoration should not be forgotten. At one time these would never have been considered subjects for flower arrangements, but today *pot-et-fleur,* or the arrangement of cut flowers and potted plants together, is a style of decoration which is growing in popularity, something which pleases me greatly since I introduced it. (There is an example of *pot-et-fleur* on the cover and also in *Flowers You Buy.*) Good, long-lasting pot plants are now available to everyone and in ever-increasing variety. While some of them can be expected to last for years, even those kinds whose lives are more fleeting nevertheless last longer than cut flowers, especially in centrally heated homes.

From *pot-et-fleur* it is not a great step to plant arrangement, an art which on a grandiose, over-lavish, and somewhat tasteless scale was practised by the Victorians and possibly because of their over-indulgence has tended to be forgotten since their time. Today compositions consisting entirely of growing plants, newly planted or remaining in their pots, are playing a role of increasing decorative importance.

Many of the so-called foliage plants have leaves as bright as any flower. Those who live in towns or have no gardens would do well to consider these as components of 'flower' arrangements. Those with gardens, greenhouses or some other suitable place to raise house-plants will find it both possible and profitable to build up a stock from which a never-ending succession of home decorations can be made.

Those who regret that flowers when cut are often so fleeting, and who perhaps because of this might be reluctant to spend time on flower arrangement proper, may find a greater pleasure and satisfaction in the arrangement of the entire living plant rather than its part. Like the traditional flower arrangement this form of decoration also offers a great deal more than appears on the surface. It has a particular appeal for those with 'green fingers'.

2 PRINCIPLES OF DESIGN

While today's styles of arrangement differ so much from east to west, these are obviously the product of gradual evolution in the art, because examples of very early flower arrangements in almost any country, including Japan, do not differ so greatly from each other. To modern eyes many of them appear over-massed and lacking in form. The containers are heavy and dominant; there is no recurring pattern.

It is natural enough that the materials should be tightly massed in these early arrangements, for without efficient stem holders how else could the decorator make them stand in place? Except by bunching them and inserting the stems in an aperture just large enough to hold them, few flowers could have been massed and kept alive for longer than a few hours. Sometimes stems were arranged in damp sand rather than plain water, and sometimes flowers were placed in containers, often baskets, filled with damp moss, but this was mainly to supply moisture rather than for support.

One can often see therefore why even short stems were arranged in tall vases, a fashion incidentally that has lasted up to the present day. If containers are light in weight and the flowers inexpertly arranged they tend to overbalance. Once flower arrangement became more sophisticated and means of holding the flowers just where the decorator wanted were introduced, vessels became shallower.

Bunched or posied

When the means to hold stems securely in place were provided, definite patterns began to emerge. As explained earlier, originally and particularly when intended for home decoration, the flowers would first be bunched or posied. The bunch would be domed or cone-shaped and usually furnished with an outer collar of leaves or fern fronds.

Stems were left as long as possible in the bunch but for arrangement these would be cut as required, they would be cut short to fit a low bowl or left longer if the flowers were to be stood in a taller but still heavy vase, with a wide base to prevent it from overbalancing.

The leafy collar protruded over the rim of the container and thus the bunch 'sat' on the rim of the vessel. Often the tall vases had a slim waist.

This meant that they could be used for bunches with varying thicknesses of stem portion. Until the 1940s this style of vase was being produced in great numbers and can still be found, often in cut glass. It is used also at flower shows for displaying blooms such as sweet peas.

The waisted shape is seldom used for modern flower arrangements simply because it is not designed for them. It limits the arranger who finds that when side stems are arranged to suit the line of the wide base of the vase arrangements tend to be too tall or too wide. Apart from that, nipped-in containers are notoriously difficult to use, although these can be attractive (see picture on page 17; in this case the vase is modern, but its shape is similar to the old types).

1 The half-sphere: the main stems defining the design are roughly the same length. **2** The long low arrangement: the central stem is much shorter than the long side stems. **3** The circular outline: the lowest stems flow below rim level. **4** Byzantine cone: the stems grow shorter and shorter as they reach rim level.

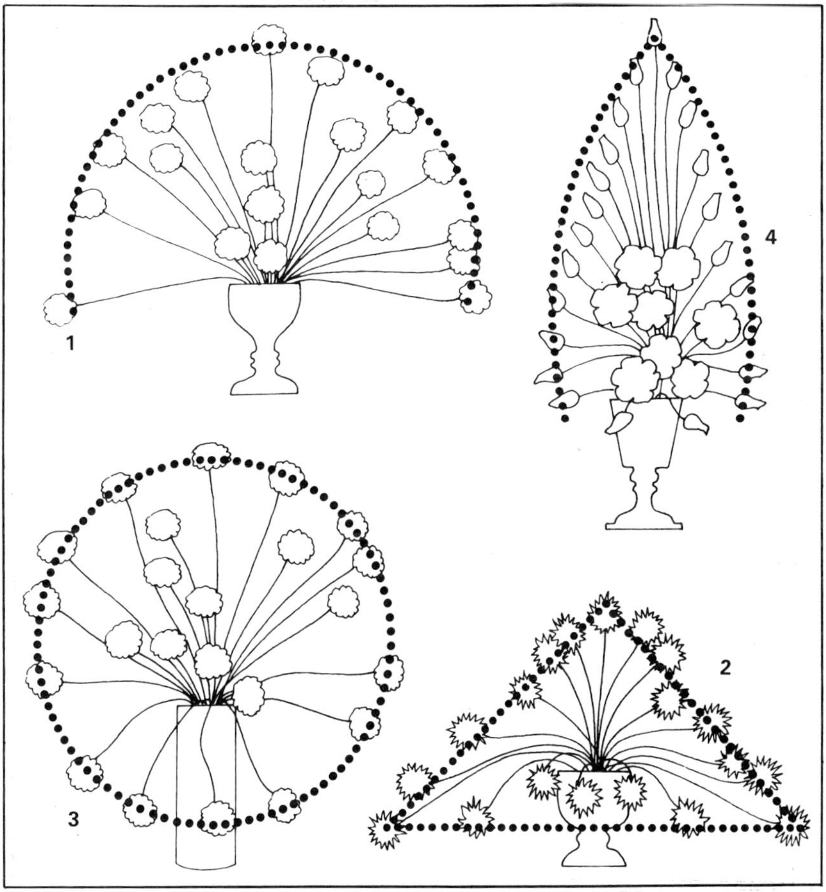

THE ALL-ROUND DESIGN

Once a way of holding individual stems was discovered the tied bunch gradually disappeared. Flowers and other materials were arranged individually, but because both the round and the cone-shaped bunches or posies were generally such pleasing and practical shapes for table centre flowers, the pattern prevailed. It is now known as an 'all-round' design. This means that it is arranged so that it looks well when viewed from all angles. Although this is a traditional style, it is an essential one to perfect, whatever your inclinations, because it underlies many other types of arrangement from Christmas decorations to Byzantine cones.

Sometimes flowers are massed almost as tightly as once was the custom, but generally speaking in an all-round arrangement each flower is given its own living space. Consequently we use fewer and see more of them.

The rules of this style of arrangement are constant. The main feature is a central stem or axis with all the other stems radiating from it as though they were the spokes of a wheel. You can vary the basic pattern as much as you will (see diagrams on page 15). To make a taller, shorter, wider, longer, flatter type of arrangement you merely vary the lengths and the proportions of the centre and side stems according to what is required. The intermediate stems will follow the outline logically.

It takes only the slightest adaptation to change the dome or half-sphere to a cone. The centre stem is elongated. It really is very simple.

A fact which is not always immediately apparent to the beginner is that many stems in an arrangement have to be shortened if they are to be arranged just as you would like to see them. Some people are reluctant to cut long stems, especially with bought flowers, but it is not possible to arrange them attractively unless some are shortened.

Building it up

The step-by-step pictures on page 18 show the method of arranging an all-round design. For the true beginner I recommend that the bowl in which the flowers are to be arranged is regarded as a clock face. The central stem is the very centre of this face and must be vertical. Next arrange the first two side stems by placing one at 3 o'clock and another opposite at 9. Then turn the bowl and arrange two more stems, one at 6 o'clock and another at 12.

The first two define the length of the arrangement and these two stems should be of equal length. The second two define the width and although they again should be of equal length they need not be so long as the first two. Very often you want a bowl to follow the line of a table rather than to occupy a precise circular area in its centre. These four stems should be at right angles to the central pivot, the vertical stem. Others arranged later can flow lower. Next fill in the other 'hours' with 1, 2, 4, 5, 7, 8, 10, and 11. None of these should protrude beyond the first stems arranged. By this time the area around the rim of the bowl should be furnished and a good start has been made on the arrangement.

Other stems should now be arranged so that they fill the area from the tip of the central stem to the rim of the container. It is most important if the arrangement is to be well balanced and symmetrical that no stem other than the first, central one is vertical. Every other stem should lean away from this important centre stem to a greater or lesser degree, and no stem should be taller than the centre.

A good move at this point is to adjust the bowl so that you have the centre and the first two side stems which you arranged in profile. Arrange a stem halfway between them. This should lean at roughly 45° from the

Waisted vases are not easy to use but can look graceful. Here, the wire netting stem-holder filled the upper portion of the vase only. The Michaelmas daisies and gentians were first arranged, central hydrangeas and delphinium florets last.

1

2

3

1 The first stages for a traditional arrangement. The central stem acts as an axis from which all other stems should radiate. **2** As they are placed in position, all the other stems should lean away from the central stem to a lesser or greater degree, the angle being widest at the base. **3** Some of the materials should always flow over the rim and at lower levels than this to avoid a hard line at rim level.

centre. Arrange another on the opposite side of the bowl in the same way. Then place intermediate stems between these. Now give the bowl a quarter-turn and repeat the process. Then turn it again and so on until the main shape is defined. You can then fill in with shorter stems or leaves should this be necessary. As you become more proficient you will find your own short cuts to easier arrangement and effective results, but once again, you must remember to keep the central stem the tallest.

These directions are for a formal arrangement which when finished resembles roughly a half-sphere, an arrangement within a semi-circular outline. This theme lends itself to many variations.

Tips for all-round arrangements: Here are some points which you may find helpful. To insert flower stems easily, hold them near the base and not near the bloom. If a stem curves (always look for the slightest curve in any stem) exploit it and see that this curve flows away from the straight centre stem. If all the stems are slightly curved make the central stem 'vertical' by placing its tip over its base. If flowers face one way, like narcissi for example, let them have their backs to the centre.

Try to create the effect that all the materials flow from one central point, the point immediately around the base of the vertical stem. Obviously you will not be able to fix all the stem bases in that small area but if when you are arranging them you point them in that direction you will achieve that effect. Any stems which have to be crossed should be crossed only below rim level. Never complete one side of an all-round arrangement first; keep turning the container and you will get a well-balanced design.

Although I have referred to a bowl, the container does not necessarily have to be round. In the chapter on *Flowers You Buy* you can see illustrations of a table centre which is made in a trough-shaped container like a ginger-bread tin. It is possible to make round arrangements in rectangular troughs, although as a rule these are best to use if you intend to elongate the half-sphere to make a half-oval.

Origin of the modern 'faced' style

Although so far only the formal tied bunches or posies which once formed the basis of home decoration have been mentioned, there was another style which also was popular. Certain flowers would be arranged in a bunch with a flat back, a sheaf. The flowers often rested against a backing of fern fronds and grasses or neat, flat branches of foliage such as beech. Such sheaf arrangements faced one way, unlike the posies which were the original all-round arrangements. Where the latter were suitable for table centres, the former were better fitted for a side table. The same type of vases were used for sheaves because they also had a thick stem portion.

In spite of popular taste, which was guided no doubt mainly by economy, there were those who, because they always had plenty of flowers at their disposal, continued to use an all-round arrangement in preference to the sheaf, even if the flowers were stood against a wall and a greater part of the arrangement was hidden. Although there are times when such an

Wild flowers in an informal arrangement based on the traditional bowl, the stems held on a large pin-holder. The dandelions are arranged while the clocks are still immature.

arrangement might be appropriate—at Christmas, for instance, when an arrangement based on a conifer shape is stood on a sideboard—today this seems extravagant and slightly ostentatious. Instead we make 'faced' arrangements to decorate those many areas in a room where a container can be stood close to a wall. If we are to accept that, basically, flower arrangement can be defined as displaying flowers to their fullest value, then it follows that there is no decorative point in wasting half of those in any arrangement by putting them out of sight.

SYMMETRICAL TRADITIONAL DESIGNS

There are many styles of faced arrangements and they carry us into oriental arrangement as well as to that which has originated in other parts of the world, as we shall see. But first let us move easily and logically from the traditional all-round arrangement to another type, the symmetrical traditional arrangement, which in this case is really little more than an all-round arrangement split down the centre.

This is an extremely useful style. The flowers can be arranged in a very simple manner or they can be given the full treatment and the arrangements used for weddings and other special occasions. Simple adaptations can be made to create delightful Christmas decorations based on the outline of a Christmas tree. Matching pairs of arrangements, pedestal decorations, *pot-et-fleur*, plant arrangements, are just some that can be based on this style.

Method of working: As before, we begin with the centre stem, for the important thing about these arrangements is that they should be evenly balanced. In its new role this stem still has the leading part to play, but now, instead of standing it vertically in the very centre of the container, we push it as far back against the rim as it will go, still as a central point and still vertical. By doing this we provide maximum space for the flowers to be arranged. It also makes the ensuing stages much easier. So far as actual arrangement is concerned the method and the principles are much the same as those we discussed earlier. The difference now is that we are concerned with showing only the 'face', as it were, and not the back of the 'head'.

The centre stem still defines the height. The two side stems still go at right angles to it and these still define the width of the arrangement. Instead of placing other stems all around the rim, as recommended for the bowl arrangement, the next move is to arrange intermediate stems between the tallest and the side stems. Once again, these should not stand higher than the centre stem, nor wider than the side stems. Their tips will sketch the outline of the proposed shape. This can be softly rounded or pyramidal. Shape is determined by the lengths of these early stems.

If the stems which are placed at right angles to the centre, whether in this or an all-round arrangement, are stiff and straight there is likely to be a harsh and ugly line at the lower part of the arrangement. Fortunately, often a flower has a straight lower portion of the stem and a curving upper part, so that if the lower portion is arranged at right angles to the centre stem this problem does not arise, if you remember to let curves flow away from the centre.

If the stem is straight, or nearly so, for its entire length, then more curving, shorter stems should be arranged below it to make a softer line. Stems which curve lower than the two main side stems can accentuate the shape of the outline of the arrangement. Often a semi-circular outline can be extended by these lower stems so that it is possible to imagine the arrangement inside an oval outline.

Linking container and flowers: Symmetrical traditional arrangements tend to have fairly conspicuous containers. Sometimes these too are traditional and deserve to be seen but this is not always the case. Often we make modern arrangements which are merely following the traditional concept. In a low arrangement made either in the all-round style or in this faced style under discussion, the container tends to be hidden by the lowest stems. In some cases this is a good thing because it means that we can use many objects of little value or beauty as containers. In all taller arrangements the container tends to become more conspicuous. This subject is discussed at greater length in *Choosing your Container* but meanwhile it must be stressed that the container should never dominate the flowers. Both should appear as a unity, so it is important to link one with the other in some way.

Usually all that is necessary, apart from the choice of colour and texture, is to carry on the line of the arrangement so that it tapers off prettily and does not come to an abrupt halt. It is also important to arrange the lowest stems so that they flow over the rim of the container to a greater or lesser degree, according to their character, in order to give a third-dimensional effect to arrangements. If this is not done, apart from the flowers appearing to have no connection with the container, the arrangement itself might have a flat, uncontoured appearance.

When you select materials for arrangement, especially if you cut your own, set aside those with extra curving stems or even floppy flowers (so long as these are in good condition) for this purpose. When you cut the laterals or side stems from any branch such as blossom, foliage, berries, seed heads, where possible cut them always with an inch or more of the main stem still attached. This will help you arrange a stem at an angle which would be difficult to achieve otherwise. For instance, when you insert the little piece of main stem down into the container its lateral will flow away from it over the rim of the container quite easily.

How to get a good 'profile'

It is apt that this style should be called a 'faced' arrangement because to make it really attractive and appealing it needs to have good features. To achieve this take care that the carefully arranged flowers are not so precise that they end up as a unit that is flat and uninteresting, a face with no character in other words.

Begin by making a good 'profile'. Having arranged the first definitive stems at the back of the container well against the rim, or as near to it as possible, turn the container so that the central, vertical stem is to your left or right. Now arrange the next stems so that they show the side view of the arrangement. Just in the same way as the stems were placed in the all-round arrangement, so should these also lean away from the central stem to a lesser or greater degree according to their height; less at the top, where the tall stems are near the tip of the central stem, roughly at right angles when shorter or shortened stems are at, or near, rim level and at a greater angle still if they flow over the rim and point downwards. At the same time, do not make an unbroken central line of blooms. Alternate them slightly and mix materials

1 The bowl complete with holder, in this case a large pin-holder, stands on a piece of gold paper. The fruit is arranged on this and round the bowl. **2** The flowers are arranged on the pin-holder. Some of the individual blooms are cut from the heavy clusters and arranged on their short stems. Brown turkey oak leaves frame them. **3** If the apples are mounted on wires they can be arranged in any position. A loop in the base of the wire fits between the points of the pin-holder. (See overleaf for finished arrangement.)

1

2

3

Flowers, fruits and foliage have been chosen not only because they are seasonal but also to harmonise with the china and table setting.

where this is desirable or practical. Later you can arrange others to the left and right of this central area.

When you turn the arrangement to face front once again, you may find that it is still not contoured enough (this is often the case where very uniform flowers are being arranged). If so, cut some of the stems much shorter than before and recess the blooms so that they are on a different plane from those nearest them. Cut them only one at a time so that you do not have too many too short stems on your hands; often only two or three are needed.

Tapering the edges: It is important to grade flowers in all arrangements. Naturally enough one tends to look for the longest stems to go at the back of an arrangement, but this is not enough. An arrangement should taper at its edges, which means that not only the tallest stem but also one with the smallest flower should be at the tip. Unfortunately there are always snags when one actually comes to arrange the flowers. Often, for instance, the longest stems carry the largest blooms! If the flowers are bought they are likely to be all of one size and in this case so long as the central stem has been well placed the actual shape of the arrangement will take care of its proportions. If the flowers are very formal the arrangement is improved if some contrasting material is arranged with the blooms. More of this later.

So many flower arrangements fit naturally inside a triangular outline, as this one does. The footed metal bowl holds mixed dahlias mingled with nicotiana, chicory, golden rod, escallonia blossom and other snippets.

It may seem as if there are many things to consider in these early stages, but in practice you learn very quickly and naturally to appreciate these principles of good balance and proportion. The rules given here are based on essentially practical foundations. Making a flower arrangement is sometimes like cooking a dish; you simply follow the same basic method according to what is being prepared.

Go where the flowers lead: If you begin correctly you are unlikely to go wrong later. Indeed, arrangement should be smooth and not at all time-consuming. The important feature in the type of arrangements under discussion is the centre stem. If you keep this as your guide, everything else should follow logically. Never be in such a hurry that you do not fix this firmly in place and make quite sure that it really is just as you want it before you arrange any other stems.

I began by saying that the traditional symmetrical arrangement was nothing more, really, then a half globe cut down the centre, but I know that after you have become proficient at arrangement you will not start out with a definite shape in mind but will be more inclined, as I often am, to go where the flowers lead you. You will frequently find that the flowers themselves dictate the pattern of an arrangement. By the time you have adjusted the other tall stems to suit the centre stem, placed the best flowers so that they can be seen to advantage, arranged heavier, denser material low, or brought some stems over the rim to hide the stem holder and to give a third dimensional effect, you have made the shape!

THE ETERNAL FLOWERY TRIANGLE

You are almost certain to find that many of the arrangements you begin quite casually finish up by being those whose outlines are not circular but triangular. This is really quite logical. If you follow the rule of first getting the centre stem in place and then arranging the side stems, inevitably you have described a triangle. The manner in which the intermediate stems are arranged will decide whether you go on to fill in the triangle or whether you change it to a semi-circular, ovoid or semi-oval outline.

I am continually surprised by the number of my own home arrangements which end this way and one has only to walk round an exhibition of flower arrangements to see that this is the most popular shape. I have heard it called the 'eternal herbaceous triangle'. This triangular shape must satisfy some spiritual need in us. After all, church spires and many of man's religious monuments and symbols have a triangular outline. However, the triangular flower arrangement is not necessarily traditional or symmetrical. A glance through this book will reveal many arrangements of great diversity based on this shape or which fit into a triangular outline. Compare for example the table decoration of hippeastrums and grapes on page 24 and the autumnal mixture opposite it.

The triangular outline does not necessarily have to rest on a base drawn across the rim of the container. Sometimes it may not be apparent at the first casual glance that an arrangement actually lies within a triangle, but it is surprising how often it does.

Flower arrangements in low containers tend to have to rely more on line and 'atmosphere' than do most of those in taller vessels. As a rule one finds that the 'eternal triangle' proves naturally to be the most engaging and rewarding pattern for these. This is especially so when one uses a low rectangular container because the basal line of the vessel quite naturally becomes the base of the triangle.

Influence of the container: The style of container one uses has a great influence on the style of the arrangement. It is possible to repeat the traditional patterns in other containers, to make an all-round arrangement in, say, a deep ashtray or to make a faced arrangement in an oven dish, but in either case we would be wasting the potential of both the flowers and the vessel. Being tied to one or two types of container means being restricted in the kind of arrangement one makes. The more containers at one's command the more interesting, varied and beautiful arrangements can be.

The container will also affect the proportions of a flower arrangement; these are best based on the measurement of any container taken at its broadest part. The tallest stem should never be less than one and a half times that measurement. However, sometimes, according to the materials you are using, you will find that it can be very much more and still look pleasantly in proportion.

Accent on line

Modern arrangements depend a great deal on the beauty of line as opposed to mass; the line is often accentuated. Later we shall see that in fact the appreciation of the importance of line is not really a modern attitude.

Mass arrangements are often block shapes and although the components of the arrangements can be extremely varied, one from another, there tends to be a sameness about their general appearance. They can seem static, although this is not to say that they are stiff or lifeless. Line arrangements can more easily be made to be distinctive and are often original without being stunts. The pleasant thing is that often these qualities are more effectively achieved by using proportionately fewer flowers than by using many. This means that not only are line arrangements pleasing and interesting but are also extremely practical so far as their components are concerned.

Some years ago I first showed daffodils and other types of narcissi arranged in a crescent of colour rising up from a shallow dish. This was made simply by stepping the flower heads so that one stood a little higher than the one below. It seemed to be such a pleasant and logical way, as well as a new one, of displaying a bought bunch of uniform blooms so that each one could be seen and admired and yet fit into a special and distinctive decoration. It is a style easy to do and now quite popular (see page 101).

The important thing is that it would not have been so easy to have evolved this type of arrangement without the aid of a heavy pin-holder. These are products of the east and are ancient, not modern and western as one might think. Their introduction has enabled us to use shallow con-

tainers, resulting in a tremendous change in styles of flower arrangement. (See *Preparation and Equipment.*)

THE JAPANESE INFLUENCE

Today's styles are more influenced by the Japanese than many of us realise or perhaps appreciate. To take one simple instance, as we have seen in the west we have up to now been mostly concerned with the true flower of a plant, its colour and, particularly in times past, its scent. This is what most people mean by a flower. In the Japanese language of flower arrangement the word *hana,* which we translate loosely as a flower actually means, and has meant for centuries, much more than this. It embraces all manner of materials, anything that forms or once formed part of a plant. These are those materials which are now recognised everywhere as suitable components for flower arrangements.

So much is said and written about the philosophy of Japanese arrangement and so much attention is paid (even by those who live western lives) to the ritual and etiquette which accompanies it that it is often overlooked that like many other things that have lasted for centuries it is based on plain common sense and experience. For instance, one reads, 'In arranging flowers the instruments are placed with the flowers on a tray to the right of the operator, the vase in front and the water pot to the left.' Essentially practical, surely, and just the way one would expect an efficient person to work.

Early examples of Japanese floral art reveal that they resemble those early styles made in other countries. But once ways in which stems could be held exactly and securely were devised, the old, original style, *Rikkwa,* was dropped in favour of controlled arrangements. As time went by these became more and more stylised, not only as more types of holders were introduced but as more people interpreted the basic rules in their own way.

Practical underlying the spiritual: Originally, as in all parts of the world, the arranged flowers were linked with religious ceremonies and life. In Japan they continued this way, invested with religious symbolism and spiritual interpretation. Wondering why this should be so, I can imagine how as the arranger, in this case originally a priest, became more and more successful he would seek to conceal the practical reasons for his success, a case of professional jealousy! But as a teacher he would need to pass on his methods, though probably only to a chosen few. It was essential that such simple matters should be given importance. One can see how gradually this minor art would have become invested with a shroud of mysticism.

Others followed the example and the time came when it was impossible to separate the practical from the spiritual. The Japanese evolved more and more complicated ceremonies of flower arrangement for the favoured élite and associated these with tea-making ceremonies. In time each had its own

Today's styles of flower arrangement all over the world are influenced by the classical Japanese designs.

ritual, philosophy and language. In flower arrangement the supports which held the stems, the containers, the bases on which these are set, the settings in which the completed arrangements were placed, had names known only to the initiated. It was said that this mystical art could be undertaken only by those who had engaged in long periods of training, and even before making any arrangement it was necessary to meditate for a long period.

Ikebana

Just as the western flower arrangement scene has become changed through the centuries, so has this classic and ancient style undergone certain modifications. Currently the imagination of many western arrangers is captured by *Ikebana*. But this word means simply, 'keeping cut flowers alive in water'. This is basic Japanese flower arrangement, and indeed any other kind. But at the moment it is interpreted by a host of schools and teachers in many ways. Some examples are far removed from the original classical concept. Even so *Ikebana* today is still based on certain elements of mysticism. Some exponents like to indulge in formal etiquette and the ritual procedures.

Not all those who enjoy the *Ikebana* styles of arrangement wish to embrace Japanese concepts nor to call the tools of their hobby by foreign names. Yet they see this style as eminently suitable for their purpose even when it is approached in a western manner. And so it is. If you have been inhibited from trying oriental arrangements because you feared that it was far too complicated for you, do appreciate that many people take as few minutes over making one of these arrangements as there are flowers in their container. It is a very simple matter to fit *Ikebana* into a busy contemporary life; you need no philosophy, no periods of contemplation or meditation, just the sound common sense that inspired the movement in the first place.

But so that you can judge for yourself whether or not a little mysticism is worthwhile, here are the fundamental rules of ancient Japanese flower arrangement.

Symbol of heaven: The basic shape is an irregular triangle which is formed by three stems known as *shushi*. It is permissible to use more than three stems and these additional stems are known as *jushi*, but they should always be under the domination of the three main stems. These are said to signify heaven, earth and man, and are known as *shin*, *soe* and *hikai*.

Shin is of the greatest importance and is always the tallest. Ideally, and following the classic interpretation, this stem should be curved, a quality not always to be found if one has to rely on bought, uniform flowers. Its tip should always be over its base. This is an example of the solid good sense of these rules, for if the arranger sees that the tallest stem stands this way it can lead only to a well-balanced design.

Sometimes, and especially if the arranger has been able to select and gather the materials rather than buy them, a stem will be very curving. It is still possible to arrange it so that it is allowed to undulate, yet its tip must return to base. Often to follow this rule all that is necessary is simply a matter of arranging the lower part of the stem well away from the vertical.

In Japanese arrangements many stems are artifically induced to assume the correct curves.

Earth and man: The *soe* is the stem next in importance. This should always be placed to the side of the main stem and the two should appear to rise together from the surface of the water. After a while *soe* follows an independent course. It should never be more than two-thirds the height of the main stem.

Hikai, as befits man, assumes a lowly position in this floral trinity. This short stem should be one-third the length of the second stem. It should flow forward, thus giving the arrangement a third dimension. However, it should not assume a drooping position and should never be allowed to rest on the rim of the container.

There are practical reasons for this, for by so doing one ensures that a siphon is never formed. This can be a nuisance and it is easy to cause a siphon without realising what is happening. Should there be a woolly leaf in the arrangement, half in water and half out, it will act as a wick, transferring the water over the rim and emptying the container drip by drip. This is one reason why in all kinds of arrangements one should strip the foliage from the portion of stem which is to go under water.

The additional stems

The *jushi* should always be added last if they are used at all. Usually three or five are sufficient. They are said to symbolise water, fire, wood, metal and the soil. These stems must always be shorter.

Great emphasis is laid on the importance of water in the container. This is considered to be an integral part of any arrangement because it represents the soil or earth from which the plants grew in the first place. Because of this in Japanese arrangements many vessels are used in which the water is plainly visible. At one time this was one of the greatest differences between western and oriental arrangements. Now a collection of shallow containers is a part of every keen flower arranger's equipment.

It is also important that the stem ends, though not their bases, are visible. They should flow close together as they rise from the water. This is said to symbolise the manner in which a plant springs from the soil. Obviously this means that stem-holders must be both efficient and inconspicuous, or capable of being made so; fortunately there is a wide range of holders on the market. It also means that stems must sometimes be pruned, shaped or coaxed so that they follow the required line.

Special bases: The finished arrangement should always stand on a base. There are many truly lovely Japanese objects made for this purpose, some of them collectors' pieces. Here once again is evidence of common sense. Often condensation will be formed under a water-filled container if this is not absolutely waterproof and this damp would damage the furniture. However, apart from its original purpose, the base in an oriental arrangement has become an integral part of the whole.

Those who would like to adopt the custom for use with modern western arrangements (and there is much to commend it) will find that many everyday objects make splendid bases, mats and trays and even teapot stands among them. It is also possible to buy specially-made bases from shops which supply *Ikebana* enthusiasts.

Learning from the Japanese

The foregoing is a very potted résumé of the thoughts behind Japanese flower arrangement, for I have touched only on the fundamentals. The interpretation by the different schools of thought down through the ages and their contribution to the evolution of modern flower arrangement is outside the scope of this book. But before we leave the subject for the present, it is worth considering some of the lessons that can be learnt from Japanese flower arrangement.

Firstly, it is clear that it is not necessary to have a great many flowers or other materials to make beautiful and satisfying decorations. In classic Japanese arrangement no superfluous materials were permitted. By arranging them to numbers, as it were, every piece of material had its place and its purpose. Restraint was shown to be both beautiful and desirable and asymmetry depended upon balance.

A traditional practice which appeals to me was that of first taking the materials in the hand and holding them as they would be displayed in the container. This preliminary step can save a great deal of time when arrangements of many kinds are being made. This practice can be taken further and one can completely arrange and then tie the flowers before inserting them into the container. This is an ideal way of using bottle-shaped containers and it can be applied to materials of many kinds from snowdrops to sticky buds.

Proportions and placement: Another golden rule was laid down by one Yurasaki, 'Never decide on the flower vessel until you have seen the flowers.' On the face of it this seems self-evident but there must be many of us who set out, say, to find berries and foliage to fill a certain favourite container. Japanese rules help the undecided and I think that some are worth observing in the beginning for many styles other than the Japanese. Later one can find one's own way.

Take the rule relating to the stem proportions for tall vases. The ancient masters said that the tallest stem should be as long as the height of the vase plus its width at the widest part plus half this sum again. Classically it can be more than this, but it should never be less. A simpler working calculation would be to say that the tallest stem, measured upwards from rim level, should be roughly one and a half times the height of the container.

When I described the all-round and the faced arrangements I stressed the importance of the centre stem and suggested that one should regard this as the axis around which the other materials should revolve. But not all arrangements lend themselves to the central stem rule. In this case we have to imagine a line which will take its place and become the centre of balance. This will give a guide to both proportions and placement of materials.

The lovely 'Lazy S' line is one of the most delightful designs in flower arrangement. A few single chrysanthemums cut from a long stem make a firm S inside a frothy mass of guelder rose.

THE LAZY 'S'

For the moment let us step right away from the triangles, half-spheres and semi-circles to one of the loveliest of lines, sometimes known as 'the Hogarth curve', after the artist. American flower arrangers call it 'the Lazy S', which seems to me to be as good a description as any. It is formed by fitting flowers into an S-shaped line, which may be very pronounced or it may be long drawn out, but in either case there will be no well-defined, tall, central stem. An example of an S-line arrangement is shown on page 33.

This is a line which, apart from its beauty, is also useful for arranging several flowers of the same kind, which means that it suits bought flowers well. It is very effective either used on its own or when it is used as an 'embroidery', a pattern within a shape. For example, one can use a framework of foliage—say, a flat and beautifully shaped branch of beech—and apply an S of summer daisies down its centre and over the rim. In winter one can make a wide arrangement of evergreens and use an S of very few flowers to bring in colour. There really is no limit to the number of improvisations; the line need not always remain a precise S, but can be more serpentine if this seems desirable.

Planning the design: Before arranging the flowers in this style, try to imagine a line running down through the centre of the container and extending well above it. Flowers can then be arranged to the left or right of it so that the S cuts through it. They will then be balanced though not necessarily equal. The two parts of the S need not be the same length any more than they are when we write the letter by hand. The shape will depend very much on the height of the container.

An S can be made so that its tip touches the top of an imaginary vertical line on the left and its base reaches to the end of the imaginary line on the right, or vice versa. But this is not an inflexible rule; the S can often be pivoted with attractive results. The point where the line of the S crosses the imaginary central line will be the focal point and here it is that one should arrange the greatest mass of materials.

This is all much simpler to do than it sounds. Take a spring flower arrangement as an example. In a tall vase you can arrange a curving stem of blossom perhaps, coaxed to curve a little more and perhaps pruned so that its curve is accentuated. This forms the top portion of the S. Another curving piece is arranged at rim level to flow out and down, with the container behind it to form the other part of the S; this need not be equal to the top part. At the focal point a posy of primroses is arranged, a few flowers and perhaps a leaf or two leaving the round outline of the posy to follow the line of the S for a little way upwards or downwards. In this way one portion is linked with another and the S line is created.

Containers for S-line styles: This is a good line to use for tall, slim, glass containers. The stem holder can be fixed in the mouth of the vase so that it does not pass down inside the container and become visible; the mass of flowers at rim level eventually hides every trace of it and at the same time forms an integral part of the arrangement.

As a rule, S-line designs look best in tall containers and slim vessels in particular, but it depends mainly on what materials are being used. This rule can often be broken, for instance one can inscribe an S of tiny flowers across a background of foliage in a low arrangement. This line can also be used in other ways, for example, outside the container when a swag of foliage and flowers is used to decorate a table. Here often an S across the centre, or alternatively along the diagonal, can look more attractive than a straight line.

There are really no hard and fast rules about asymmetrical designs other than how they relate to containers, and even then this is a matter of personal taste. For instance, there is something inept about asymmetry in a formal symmetrical container, such as a wide urn with prominent handles. These arrangements are particularly suited to containers whose beauty of texture, design or ornament should not be cloaked with flowers. Here an S can both enhance and indicate particular features of the vessel.

Other asymmetrical styles

Asymmetrical designs of other kinds are delightful in low containers, as the Japanese have shown, and these can be used in many different ways. Simple decorations based on line arrangements can be used to tell a story, to make a nature picture or to evoke a mood or atmosphere for a special occasion. These are specially rewarding in winter and early spring when the fact that so few flowers are needed in such arrangements is a great advantage.

There is something extremely satisfying on a dull winter's day, to search the garden, hedgerow or common for materials—a branch or two of some brave, burgeoning shrub, a windfallen branch of larch cones, a coloured leaf even if it comes only from the outside of a cabbage, a mossy stone or two—and then to take just a few blooms (even those from a house-plant if no others are available) to add a note of floral colour to the collection. From this handful of such simple ingredients it is possible to create a picture, a still life which can be the essence of the season.

Those who enjoy modern settings may like to experiment with abstract arrangements. Here again one describes the style of the arrangement with the minimum of materials. The voids remaining, the spaces between two stems for example, are the shape and the body of the arrangement. These are arrangements from which as much as possible is abstracted and yet the result is pleasing and evocative.

Many arrangements consist of patterns applied to patterns. One might make a background triangular in shape, of some long-lasting foliage perhaps, and on this arrange brighter or contrasting materials inside an outline of a different shape. Sometimes this is done with intent, but often one finds that it has happened quite naturally. It is a style worth studying, especially if you are an arranger who has to buy flowers.

LEARNING TO HANDLE COLOUR

Some understanding of the colour spectrum is necessary for the flower arranger, and indeed, if you are hoping to exhibit in a flower arranging competition it is essential to understand colour terms and apply them correctly.

If we look at the rainbow we can trace the sequence of colours as they occur naturally: red, orange, yellow, green, blue and purple. Look again at orange, green and purple and you will see that they are made by the overlapping of red and yellow, yellow and blue and blue and red. You cannot make red, yellow or blue from any other colours, which is why they are known as primary colours; those that are made by mixing two primaries together, orange, green and purple, are called secondary colours.

If we continue looking at the rainbow we see that there is a point in the centre of the colour band where the colour is definite; it changes as it goes towards the neighbouring colours on each side. So we get red veering towards orange or purple; orange becoming redder or more yellow; yellow becoming more orange or green; green becoming yellow-green or blue-green, and blue veering from green to purple. These nuances are the 'hues' of a colour.

If you find it difficult to grasp the distinction between true colours and hues, take a look at a wood on a hillside. At one quick glance the wood is green. But if you take your time, look more closely and analyse what you see, you will find that the green is really made up of many different greens, yellow-green, blue-green, dark green, light green, olive green, even brown-green. These are hues.

Tones, tints and shades: Hues are often confused with tones. Tones deal with the richness of the same colour. Tints and shades depend on light and shade or shadow. It is often confusing the way we all use the term 'shade' in general conversation. 'Pastel shades' is a contradictory term. Shade is a colour or hue that has black or grey, shadow, added to it. Tints are colours or hues with light or white added. To take a homely example, think of raspberries, purple, red and cream, creamy white. Squash them together and you get a tint of the true raspberry hue.

Colours which are near each other on the rainbow we call 'analogous' or nearly related. To make colour easier to relate we curve the rainbow so that the red is next to the purple and to make things easier still we put the colours into a continuous colour wheel, each primary colour opposite a secondary. There is a natural reason for this, because complementary colours are what the brain offers when the eyes become tired. For example, if you look for a long time at a red spot and then turn away and look at a blank wall you will see a similarly shaped green spot take its place in your vision. The same thing happens with the other colours.

Natural colour harmonies

But how does all this affect the flower arranger? Complementary colours make delightful natural colour harmonies and exciting flower arrangements. They might sometimes be too bright for some furnishing schemes, but they can be adapted easily. For instance you might like to change bright yellow and purple for pale cream and mauve, or orange and blue for apricot and pale blue, or holly berry red and green to pink and apple green. Also in harmony are any hues of one colour. One can spend a fascinating hour collecting bits and pieces from the garden or hedgerow for arrangements of this kind.

Analogous colours, that is those which are near each other on the colour wheel, occur in many garden flowers in their natural mixtures, which is a great help to the arranger. Fuchsias, pelargoniums, sweet williams, nasturtiums, sweet peas, candytuft and roses are everyday examples. This is why their bright colours do not clash discordantly, no matter how mixed they might be.

Something very interesting happens when you mix the complementaries—borrow the children's paints and see for yourself. Mix the purple of pansies with the yellow of the same flower and you will get 'pansy brown'. Look at mixed pansies and you will find this same brown in many of the flowers. In some it will be lighter than in others, perhaps tan or ginger.

Another kind of brown is made by mixing red and green. Christmas cards, decorations and even Yule logs (the cake kind!) often successfully combine brown, green and red. No wonder, since there is such an affinity between these colours. You will get yet another kind of colour if you mix orange and blue, and more from other mixtures. Look around at some natural colour combinations and see what happens when you mix them. And don't stick to flowers. One of the most fascinating discoveries I made was when I mixed the lovely magenta and jade green of a pigeon's throat. What did I get? Warm pigeon grey!

'Broken' colours: We call all of these 'broken' colours and the reason why they are important to the decorator is because they are safe. If you are not sure what colour container to use for your flowers, or even for your room, look around. You may have one of the broken colours of either the flowers you hope to use or perhaps of your main wall or curtain colours. Put the other way around, your carpet may be one special kind of grey and you may have wondered what flowers to use with it to give the best effect. What kind of grey is it? Spend a little time with the paint box and do a little detective work. You can then make harmonies of the colours which are mixed to your heart's content.

Inspiration often comes from the flowers themselves. It really is surprising how many colours there can be in one bloom. They will always give you a guide if you spend a few moments looking at them. For instance, if you have a few tulips and wonder what colour the vase or the other plant materials should be, you can take your cue not only from the flower's colour, the hue of leaf or stem, but also from the other colours deep down inside the flower.

Furthermore, all flowers have some green in them somewhere and this links all kinds of colours, tones and hues in a lovely, natural manner. And do remember that if at any time you are in doubt as to what colour to use, all-green arrangements can be both very beautiful and economical. There is an example of such a monochrome design on page 88.

3 CHOOSING YOUR CONTAINER

For years, even centuries, people never considered arranging flowers in anything other than vessels specially designed to hold them. Indeed, there have been eras when a great deal of contemporary art was engaged in the production of beautiful vases of china, glass and metal for this purpose and so lavish were they that many of them still can stand alone, without flowers, delightful decorations in their own right. In fact the vases became so gorgeous that they dominated the flowers. This no doubt was one factor in the cause of their decline in popularity.

It was the custom that flowers and vases or special flower bowls went together. Nothing else would do. Even pitchers, in which wild and garden flowers and foliage look so delightful and which now seem old fashioned though still acceptable, were once considered 'modern' and a trifle daring and unconventional by some people.

Now we are much less rigid in our attitudes, so much so that only a few of the vessels that many modern flower arrangers use were originally intended to hold flowers. Today almost anything is acceptable so long as it is waterproof and suits both its contents and its setting.

Obviously the most important thing is that any container should be capable of holding sufficient water to nurture the flowers, and it is this fact that has had such a restricting influence on flower arrangement. Because it has always been assumed that the more water we could give flowers the longer they would last, traditional vases tend to be large, often much too ungainly for modern homes if they are to be used as was originally intended. However, it has been proved that once the materials have been prepared and are turgid (that is, firm and tense by distension with water), deep water is not essential for them. In fact too great a depth of water will shorten the lives of some flowers such as sweet peas and gladioli. And so long as the stem base is never allowed to become dry it would appear that in some cases the continual evaporation of moisture immediately around the flowers is as beneficial as static water.

Using shallow containers

Those who have not yet begun to build up a collection of containers need not go to great expense. They are likely to find that there are many everyday things as well as pretty ornaments and bygones which seem to cry out for flowers. If these are not waterproof it is often a simple matter to make them so. A strong plastic sheet or bag, or alternatively cooking foil, to line the container and a stem-holder which will not pierce it are all that is necessary.

One needs a selection of low containers for various styles of arrangements. I find that I tend to use the shallow types more in winter than in summer and obviously the supply of materials at one's command will have some influence. A sturdy branch of sticky horse chestnut buds being forced to open needs a different container from a dainty branch of summer blossom, even though both may be roughly the same in size and shape. Textures are important and the glaze or the rough finish will make all the difference to the atmosphere of certain arrangements.

Decorations which are to remain in the centre of a table during a meal need to be low enough to allow one to see across the table. Nothing is more irritating than to have to talk round a flower piece. A low arrangement can easily be raised to bring it to the level of greater importance when the table is cleared by using a comport or cake stand to act as a pedestal.

From plates to ash trays

There are many suitable containers for this purpose, not the least of which are the vegetable dishes which are part of the table china. One of the plates can be used this way also. I use a number of plates about the house for a variety of arrangements. Many of them have subdued patterns, colours and textures which suit the flowers better than deeper containers and one can always leave a large expanse of the plate to show and so gain extra colour.

It is usually necessary to use a supplementary container with plates and similar shallow vessels. This holds the stem-holder, usually a pin-holder, and the water. Since this will not show, or should not, when the arrangement is finished, it can be quite humble. I use shallow food tins, though deep enough to hold sufficient water which is topped up daily, and wide enough to take the pin-holder.

However, because of modern introductions even this is not always necessary, for if one uses a block of water-retentive foamed plastic, such as OASIS, this can simply sit on the plate. All that is necessary is that it shall be kept moistened. A little water can be poured into the plate each day.

Many oriental styled arrangements and those which I call 'picture stories' need shallow dishes. It is possible to buy some from shops which specialise in *Ikebana* accessories, but one can equally well find them in kitchen shops or local potteries, vessels designed for food rather than flowers. Often a junk shop or stall will yield a fine selection of lidless tureens, plates and so on.

Some of my favourites are outsize ashtrays. The clean lines of modern vessels call out for individually tailored flower arrangements and are specially suitable for those who have to buy their flowers. A modern container will show off a handful of distinctive seedheads, flowers or leaves in a manner that a traditional vase seldom can equal.

Above: If a container is not waterproof, line it with a piece of plastic or cooking foil. Use a foamed plastic stem-holder in case the wire netting should pierce the lining. In this old tea-caddy are anemones, fuchsia, spindle berries, maple leaves and canary creeper. Right: The soft gleam of metal suits flowers. This sugar scoop holds a block of well-soaked foamed plastic in which the annual gypsophila and Garnette roses hold firm.

Tall and slim: So long as they stand firmly, tall slim containers are ideal for holding market flowers, those which have been mass-produced and are uniform in shape, size and length. It is usually simple to extend the top few flowers in a bunch and to adjust the others so that each bloom has its own little living space, necessary because flowers go on growing in water. All you have to do then is trim the stem ends should this be necessary and stand the bunch in the container. If the stem portion is slim and tends to lean, either use the wrapping paper screwed into a ball, placed against the back of the bunch and pushed down inside the container, or make a wedge of a piece of special foamed plastic.

When flowers are scarce these tall containers look well with one lovely branch, suitably pruned or shaped or perhaps extended into an S, supporting two, three or four flowers arranged nearer the rim and flowing out at a different angle from the branch.

Coloured glasses

A collection of glasses of many shapes and sizes will aid the arranger, for these lend themselves so agreeably to use with all kinds of plant material. A large green brandy balloon looks most attractive filled with an arrangement of green materials such as leaves, seedheads, grasses and whatever else can be found. A cluster of gleaming berries or other fruits such as little green apples will appear to have an affinity with the texture of the glass and thus makes a pleasant link between it and the other contents.

Blue glass will add a lively touch to the soft passive greys of downy stems and leaves. It will bring a sparkle to foliage which is covered with a bluish or greenish bloom and to other materials. I like to see whole plants of the annual opium poppy, *Papaver somniferum* arranged this way. Red glass can be used in winter to bring a warm note into the room and will carry its complementary greens delightfully. And if you want to make a complementary harmony it is usually easy to find flowers, anemones for example, and berries, rose hips or holly, which will match or harmonise with the glass.

Round, bulb-shaped glasses are naturally suited to those flowers which grow from bulbs. If the aperture is narrow enough sometimes all one needs is three daffodils with five or so of the green, spear-shaped leaves behind them, both flowers and foliage arranged so that one towers a little way above the one below. Nerines, irises and freesias look lovely displayed this way and it is such an easy method of arrangement.

Quite often you will find that it is best to arrange the stems in the hand and tie them together before inserting them into the glass. This, incidentally, is a method I use when arranging flowers in bottle-shaped containers. Indeed I have several true bottles which once held drinks (liqueur bottles are usually the most attractive shapes) which I use throughout the year as containers.

Simple table centres

A plain glass bowl can make a lovely and unusual table centre, the arrangement of which need take no longer than a few minutes. All it needs is a cluster of flowers and a few leaves arranged in just one area at rim level, like the decoration on a hat. The stems are held in a small ball of crumpled wire netting hooked by its own cut ends on the rim of the bowl. (Transparent sticky tape on the outside of the bowl can also be used for this purpose.) The stems are inserted through the mesh into the water. Only a few flowers are necessary, say five roses and a little of their own foliage, or five daffodils and variegated ivy leaves, or one lovely dahlia framed with foliage and berries.

There are variations to be played on this theme. Shallow dishes or deep plates of ceramic, metal or what you will can also be ornamented with a floral 'knot' according to season or where they are to be placed. While some of these containers may not look as lovely as glass when filled with plain water, there are other things they can hold, such as green bun moss in the spring to complement a group of early flowers or blossom, or even an assortment of leaves. The stems of all these can go under the moss into the water, or alternatively into foamed plastic, attractive pebbles, seashore stones, seashells, aquaria stones, marbles or beads. All of these can play a part and present an interesting expanse of material within the walls of the container which adds another quality of texture, colour or atmosphere. It can be very rewarding to experiment with some of these unusual accessories.

Metal containers

Flowers really do live longer in vessels made of metal. Bacterial activity in the water inside metal containers is much less than in water held in other materials; it is highest in clear glass. This means that the water in metal keeps sweet longer.

However, this depends upon the cleanliness of the container. If a glass container is dirty on the inside then it is clearly visible, so glass containers tend to be kept clean. But a metal, pottery or china container can sometimes be put away after use without being properly cleaned and this fact can easily be overlooked when next the container is used. This can make a considerable difference to the life of your flowers, so it is worthwhile to spend just a few minutes cleaning containers meticulously after use.

Usually the shapes of metal containers tend to vary considerably from those of ceramics or glass. Metal tankards, pitchers, fruit bowls, kitchen moulds and measures can all be used for flower arrangements, although some are a little difficult to use until you learn one or two tricks of the trade. Silver, pewter, copper and brass suit flowers admirably and it is always possible to find those which match the colours of the metals. There are other metals of course and all seems grist to the flower arranger's mill. Among these others, figures in Britannia metal, and others which are often converted into containers merely by giving the figure a small vessel to hold, are also used. These tall containers give height and style to small and inexpensive flowers.

Candlestick arrangements

Another means of adding height and grace to flowers is to use candlesticks. These can be fitted with candle cups, little footed bowls which fit into the top of the candlestick in the same way as a candle. These are on sale in florist's shops and in many garden centres and department stores. The bowl is quite large enough to take plenty of flowers. It is even more accommodating if instead of wire netting or a pin-holder it holds a cylinder of OASIS which protrudes for an inch or two above the rim of the cup.

A pair of candlesticks fitted this way make delightful buffet decorations. They are attractive on a long dining table so long as they can be placed in a convenient position where they will not be in the way. One alone makes a good centre for a small table. At Christmas these candlestick arrangements look effective on a mantelshelf or sideboard, when evergreens are grouped around tall candles, their colours matching the tree baubles, berries and other ornaments arranged among the foliage to give a seasonal touch.

Right: Polyanthus and other garden flowers informally arranged are set off by the rich lustre of this handsome copper trough.

Below: These dried flowers in a copper saucepan include helichrysum, nicandra, hydrangea, dyed green gnaphalium with saponaria seed heads and preserved leaves.

4 PREPARATION & EQUIPMENT

Most keen flower arrangers end up by being collectors of some item related to the art. One can happily go on looking for the right kind of container for ever. But there are other types of equipment which once you have used you will always want again and again, in as much variety as possible.

Obviously the first in importance are stem-holders, for unless the flowers are going to stay exactly as we have placed them there is no point in spending time arranging them in the first place. Quite the most versatile and cheapest holder is wire netting of $1\frac{1}{2}$ in. to 2 in. mesh. This is important, for the smaller mesh is nothing like so malleable and not only do we want to be able to push the netting down inside any kind of vessel, but we must also be certain that it will hold slender stems yet give way to a stouter stem should this have to be inserted in the crumpled mesh.

Sometimes it is possible to buy small, narrow rolls of netting, but if you have to buy a large roll it is a good plan to share it with several other flower arrangers. The galvanised type is better than the plastic covered simply because it is not so thick. On the other hand, the covered wire will cause no damage to precious containers which must not be scratched. This wire tends to slip, even if the cut ends are hooked over the rim of the container. It is best held in place with a few strips of transparent sticky tape passed over the wire and on to the outside of the container, just below the rim, where it will not show once the flowers have been arranged. It is convenient to keep the netting inside the container for which it has been cut once this has been emptied and cleaned. This saves time and patience.

When a tall, heavy branch of blossom or foliage is arranged you will sometimes find that the container is too light and is liable to tip over, even when water has been added. When arranging materials of this kind I first half-fill the container with sand and rest the netting on this. Besides helping to adjust the balance this also aids arrangement, for the thick stem can be passed down through the netting and into the sand where it usually becomes well and truly anchored.

Using wire netting

It is always wise to measure the netting correctly because this saves one from

1

having to begin all over again which can sometimes be the case if the stems are not being held as efficiently as they should be. Generally the netting is cut only to the size of the area of a container in which water is held. When cutting netting for a tall pedestal vase cut it twice the depth of the bowl-shaped portion; usually it is safest to allow one and a half times the width. Remember that it is always better to have a little too much netting than too little, for some can easily be taken away.

Bend the netting into a U and then squash it so that it will go into the container from floor to rim. Stems are inserted through it at all angles. Pull up some of the cut ends because these can be used for several purposes. They can anchor the netting in a highly-glazed container in which it tends to slip. Or if a tall and heavy stem has to be pulled from the vertical to get the effect you want it can well be secured by these cut ends, which can be hooked around it at the point where it rises above rim level. Sometimes three or four of the cut ends are required in slightly different areas; it is surprising how effectively these will hold a really heavy stem.

Where you hope to arrange several tall, heavy stems it helps to cut a larger piece of netting than usual and to bring it above rim level at the back of the

1 When mixed materials of varying stem textures are to be used, it often helps to combine stem-holders. The pin-holder holds the tall stems of *Cornus mas* and ivy. The lusher, shorter stems of leaves and flowers can be held by the wire netting. **2** Variegated kale and snippets of tradescantia form the heart of the arrangement; large ivy leaves with sprigs of heather surround them. **3** When using glass containers, place the wire netting in the top portion only. Pull up some of the cut ends at the back to support the tallest flowers and hook more over the rim to anchor the mesh.

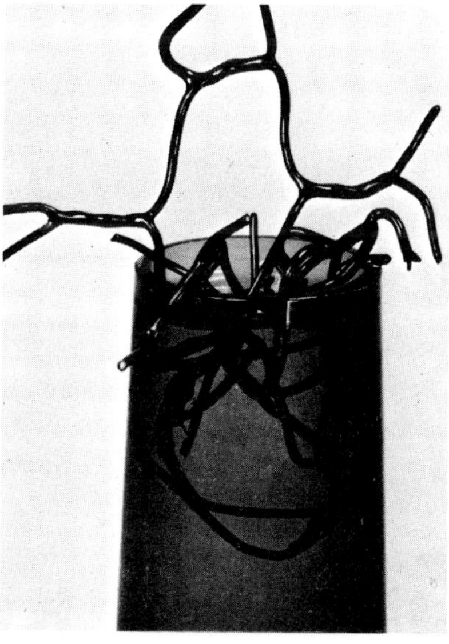

vase. The stems are then inserted through this protruding netting before they actually enter the container. They pass on down into it and are held really firmly. Other materials arranged in front of them later will hide this little piece of simple engineering.

Let the cut ends help: A similar method can be employed when the opposite types of materials, soft, floppy stems, are to be used. In this case cut a little more netting than is necessary and bring it or flute it out over the rim of the container at the front and sides. The stems can then be directed into the container but actually supported on the netting. Not a great deal of overlap is necessary, sometimes no more than 1 in., but naturally it depends upon the size of the arrangement and the materials in use. Any cut ends near the rim of the container can be used also to pin certain stems in place. They will pass without harm into the thick mid-rib of a leaf. They can be used to coax stems to hang low and to keep other pendant stems just where they are wanted. But if there seems to be no real reason to use them, just ignore them.

Once you have used netting you will grow to appreciate the many ways it can be employed to overcome certain problems. At Christmas time the same netting can be used to make foundations for garlands, swags, Christmas trees and many other topical decorations.

So far as glass containers are concerned wire netting is an essential. If a small piece of netting—a sphere or an egg, according to the shape of the aperture—is inserted into the neck of the container, it will hold a mass of stems quite well, whatever the shape and size of the container. Once again cut ends can be hooked over the rim to keep the netting well anchored. Some can be extended upwards at the back or over the sides as seen earlier.

Pin-holders

Known as *kenzan* in Japan, pin-holders are ancient stem-holders brought up to date. They come in many sizes and shapes, including minute examples for miniature arrangements or for holding a single flower. They are used mainly in shallow containers but they are also useful sometimes at the base of a tall container, especially when a tall and heavy branch is to be displayed.

These holders consist of upright pin, needle or nail points projecting upwards from a heavy metal base. Stems are impaled on the points either vertically or at an angle; woody stems are more easily arranged if the ends are cut at a slant. Plastic pin-holders are also obtainable but these will not efficiently hold all types of stems.

To prevent movement the pin-holder should be firmly anchored before starting to arrange. This is done by making four or five small pills of Plasticine or OASISFIX (a kind of sticky modelling clay) which can be lightly attached to the dry base of the holder. If this is then pressed against the floor of the container, which must also be dry, the pills will become squashed and act as washers or suckers.

A small pin-holder can sometimes be used to good effect in an unorthodox manner. If you fix it to the side of a glass container, one or several stems can be pushed against the pinpoints and held firmly in place. The pin-holder itself can be hidden with a few leaves and the stems will stand seemingly unsupported in the glass (see diagram below).

Plastic stem-holders

Now in general use, plastic stem-holders are generally types of foamed urea. They are water-retentive and yielding. So long as stems are not too soft and sappy they will enter the plastic easily and be held firmly. Only a short portion of the stem need be inserted for it to be anchored, which means that quite short-stemmed flowers can be used in a number of attractive ways. Often they can be made to appear long-stemmed.

There are two main types used for fresh flowers, OASIS and FLORAPAK. The second holds water and should not need moistening every day although it should be checked from time to time. OASIS both absorbs and releases moisture more quickly and it should not be allowed to become dry. It holds its shape well, does not easily crumble and can be used outside the container. It may also be used dry for arrangements of perpetuelles and all dried flowers. Both brands are available in the form of roughly brick-sized slabs which can be cut to shape as required. OASIS is also sold in the form of cylinders, so shaped and sized as to fit a number of useful cups, bowls, holders and other containers of various shapes, sizes and uses.

Obviously stem-holders should not be conspicuous. Wire netting inside a

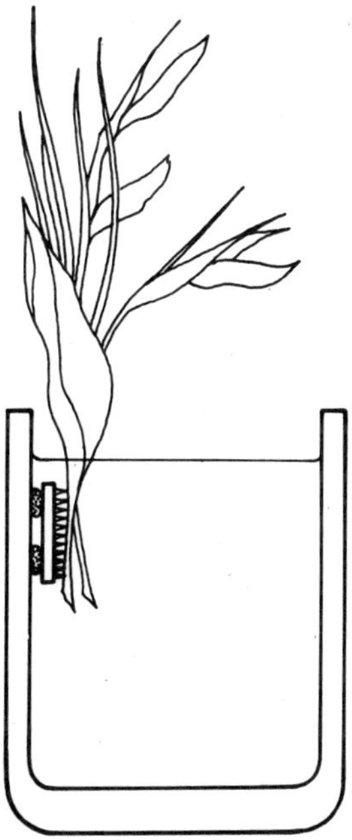

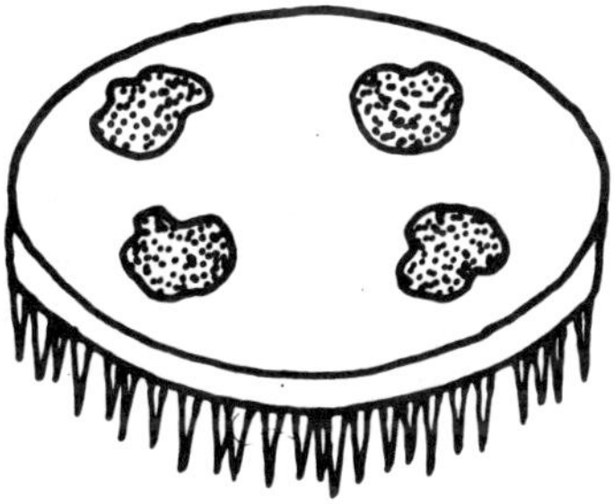

A pin-holder makes an effective stem-holder for a few flowers arranged in glass. Small pills of Plasticine make the holder adhere to the side of the container. All surfaces must be quite dry. As the flowers are arranged, their stems are pressed against the pinpoints.

container is well masked but a pin-holder or a block of plastic might easily show. Fortunately, the means we use to hide these holders also add to the interest of the flower arrangement itself and can even be an important part of it. Sometimes it may be necessary to do no more than arrange the largest flower in the group so low that it hides all trace of the holder from which it leans. Often, and this is a pretty method, a group of large leaves can be arranged like a little skirt around the base of taller stems. One can also use a mossy stone or two, a group of shells, some driftwood, fruits, a whole plant or any natural material which seems to have an affinity with the particular flowers or materials being used.

Other ways of holding stems

An enterprising flower arranger will soon discover that other types of stem-holders can be devised, according to the style of arrangement being planned. For example, in glass, so that they can show through prettily and also perhaps add a little extra colour when flowers are scarce, coloured marbles, beads, aquaria stones, small coloured pebbles and seashells can be used for firm stems or they can hide a central column of stem-holding netting or plastic.

Some stem-holders are extremely simple but have to be tailored for the arrangement being planned. These are wedges made of strips of wood or portions of twig stretched across the mouth of a container. They are useful when you want to hold just a single stem in place without its support being obvious. You can also support a few stems, in a Japanese arrangement for example, by using this method.

The Japanese used both crossed and forked sticks which they call *kubari* (see picture opposite). These are always cut from living twigs so that they are pliable. Crossed twigs are merely two pieces fastened cross-wise at the centre with raffia or twine. Naturally the finished *kubari* of either type should fit tightly into the mouth of the container and it sometimes takes a little time to determine the correct dimensions of the twigs. However, if you place a tiny piece of OASISFIX on the end of each twig you will find that it is much more likely to stay firmly in position. The stem or stems are held in one or other of the angles formed by the cross. Crossed stick *kubari* are best used if the flowers are to lean or flow out from the container.

The Y-shaped, split or forked *kubari* are made by splitting a stem just part of the way up its length. As a rule it is necessary to wedge in a little extra piece to force or keep the two arms of the Y apart. And to prevent these from splaying too far it is best to determine the required span and then bind the forked ends with raffia to keep them in place.

Making flowers last

But all this effort will not be worth while if the flowers are not long lived. The most important factor for lasting freshness is that all the materials used should be properly hardened before use. This means that all should be quite turgid and taking water well before they are placed in an arrangement.

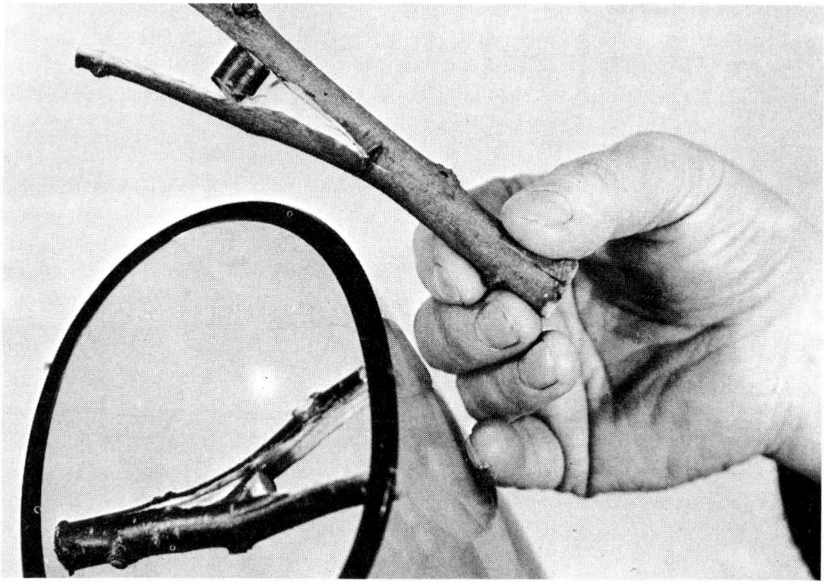

A good stem-holder, kubari, can be made from a cleft stick; this type of holder is always cut from living twigs so that they are pliable.

Part of an arranger's normal equipment should be a series of buckets or similar vessels, some deep for tall stems, some shallow to take short-stemmed flowers, for although they need a deep drink it is not wise to submerge blooms. Nor is it wise to crowd them together for this might damage some and cause others to lose much of their colour.

As soon as possible after they are gathered (or as soon as they are brought home, if bought) stand the stems in deep water. This should cover any foliage on the stems. Let them stay there for at least an hour and longer, even overnight, if possible. Plants give off water from their leaf surfaces. This is not a great problem when roots and veins are rapidly conveying it through the growing plant, but it does sometimes cause difficulties when the flowers have been cut and the roots are no longer serving the plant. By covering the leaves with water respiration is cut down and the stems will become turgid.

To ensure quick uptake of water all but hollow and very fleshy stems should be split at the base upwards ½ in. or more, according to the length of stem. This exposes the soft inner tissues. It also expels any air present which might otherwise tend to cause a lock in the stem tissues and prevent water being drawn up. To prevent flowers from wilting inexplicably (as some do after arrangement even though they have had a deep, long drink beforehand), it is advisable that the water into which they are stood for the preliminary drink should be warmed to about 70°F or 21°C. In fact I use tepid water also when I begin an arrangement and again for topping up; rain water is best.

Singeing and scalding: For a variety of materials speed and certainty of water uptake may differ widely. Some plants such as acacia or mimosa apparently cannot absorb water at all. Only humidity around the flowers and foliage keeps them fresh. You can, for example, keep mimosa fresh and fluffy for days, even weeks, if you place it under a sealed glass dome. This is a plant that is happier in a block of moist plastic than in water.

Those stems which exude a milky juice or latex, euphorbias or spurges for example, cannot take water until this flowing juice coagulates. The easiest way to hasten this is to singe the stem ends over a flame as soon as possible after cutting. Any stems which are shortened for arrangements after the singed ends have been given a drink should be re-singed. It is useful to have a candle burning nearby when using these flowers. This treatment also applies to poppies of all kinds.

Any flower which fails to become turgid when treated as above should have its stem ends stood in 1–2 in. of boiling water and allowed to remain in it until it cools, by which time it will be firm and swollen. Stem ends thus treated often become blackened and sometimes soft. This portion may be cut away if the stem has to be shortened for arrangement; once it has become turgid there should be no need to treat the new stem end. Some materials which are notorious for wilting, such as some grey or silver leaved shrubs, take water best if a little of the old wood is left on the stem. Immature tissues just do not seem to be able to drink well.

Retarding bacterial activity

Certain preservatives and nutrients are helpful to maintain freshness. There are several proprietary brands on sale. Most of these contain some glucose which seems to be appreciated by most flowers. Alternatively you can use one level teaspoon of glucose, a lump of sugar or one saltspoon of honey to a pint of water. In arrangements of fresh shrub and tree materials, especially those such as blossom in bud or Christmas evergreens which are expected to stand for some weeks, use a little of any good soluble plant food, sufficient to make a very weak solution. Since metals seem to inhibit bacterial activity, there is some validity in the old advice to place a copper coin in the container. Alternatively dropping an aspirin tablet in the water tends to discourage or delay bacterial action.

Foul water will help kill flowers and will also sometimes discolour them. So always strip the leaves from the portion of stem which is to remain under water even though it may speed up the intake of water. Avoid hammering or crushing woody and fibrous stems for the same reason. The foamed urea plastic stem-holders already mentioned contain formaldehyde which is a form of disinfectant and so these help to keep flowers fresh.

Contrary to a belief which is still widely held, flowers should not be taken from their vases each day to have a piece of stem cut away. Neither should the water need changing each day if the proper treatment has been given to the flowers. But of course the level of the water should be topped up in case it evaporates to danger level.

5 LONG-LASTING ARRANGEMENTS

While summer arrangements are often delightfully spontaneous, inspired by the flower of the moment, those for winter decoration are most successful if they are planned in advance.

For today's centrally heated houses the flower arranger needs to know of those materials which will last the winter through, which will remain decorative no matter how hot or dry the atmosphere may become. Fresh flowers cannot last long under such conditions (although there are some fresh plant materials which can be used, as we shall see) and the most reliable subjects for winter decoration are dried and preserved flowers. Since these are so varied we group them all under the omnibus heading of 'perpetuelles'.

To many people the term dried and preserved flowers still conjures up a vision of a massed muddle of faded, musty, possibly dusty everlastings. But long-lasting flowers need be nothing like this. They too can be beautiful, distinctive, ornamental, enchanting, groomed and contemporary. They can be arranged in a great variety of styles so that they suit any interior and any type of furnishing.

Furthermore, the term 'flower' taken in this context becomes stretched to its limits with fascinating results. For apart from flowers, of which many are very colourful indeed, there are fruits, plant skeletons, seed heads, fungi and others forms of plant materials in a wonderful variety, their beauty often depending more on form and texture than on colour.

Grow, buy or collect them

Long-lasting flowers are not exclusively for those who have gardens, although there are many which are easy to grow. It is well worth studying a seed catalogue for suitable subjects for the list seems to grow longer every year. Some seedsmen offer special collections of flowers for drying. There are also many plants in almost every garden, perennials, bulbs, shrubs and trees which are a source of many splendid perpetuelles. These might otherwise go unnoticed and unused, but once an arranger begins to learn about perpetuelles he or she will appreciate those that are all around. Often they are in great abundance.

Those who have no gardens will find that some flowers can be bought while others can be collected from the countryside. A walk round a country town during the summer holiday season is often rewarding, especially if it is market day. Look out for the true everlastings, helichrysums or strawdaisies, and statice, or limonium to give it its botanical name. Sometimes these can be bought in florists' shops. In early autumn you can buy physalis or Chinese lanterns and honesty.

Everlasting flowers are usually sold freshly gathered and in fairly fat bunches. If they are to be dried successfully they must be untied, the stems stripped of foliage and then retied in smaller bunches of just five or six stems. The reason for this is that small bunches allow the air to circulate more freely among and between the stems. If the foliage is not removed it is likely to become mouldy and in any case even if it should dry properly it will not be decorative.

If you want to get the most from your 'buy', the statice can first be used in fresh flower arrangements in water, and later either left in position, without water, to dry or taken out and bunched.

Drying and mounting

One should always tie all bunches tightly because as the stems dry they shrink and unless held tightly they will slip from the bunch. They should be hung, heads downwards, in a cool, dry and shady place. Never dry flowers in the sun.

Helichrysums or strawdaisies can offer problems. The flowers themselves are quite the loveliest daisies when properly dried. It would be useful if we could keep the flowers on their stripped stems. Certainly arrangement would be simpler, but it is only occasionally that this works successfully. Once dried the stems are likely to become so brittle that the heads snap off as they are being arranged. These need not be wasted, for once detached they can be mounted on false stems. Long florist's wires are best for this purpose but wiring and mounting is not easy until you have had plenty of practice. One makes a tiny hook in one end of the wire and the other end is pushed down through the centre of the daisy from above and gently pulled until the hook is embedded and almost hidden in the flower's centre.

Quite the best method is to wire and mount the flowers while they are still soft and fresh. Have ready some long florist's wires, 20 or 22 gauge as they used to be known but now classified as 0·90 mm and 0·71 mm respectively. You can buy these wires from some florists and some hardware stores. Snip most of the stem from each flower leaving just a short butt of about 1 in. Insert one end of the wire up inside the stem. It should enter quite easily if the stem is still soft and succulent. Gently but firmly push it on up into the hard centre of the flower. Do not push it so far that it comes through the centre and shows. Your flower now has a stem but it still must be dried.

If you were to tie the wires in a bundle you would bend them which is not desirable. It is much better to stand them well spread out in wide-topped containers allowing a little space between each bloom. I find the best method is to use heavy bowls or large flower pots, each filled with a block of dry foamed plastic. The wires can then be very easily spaced. Once again the flowers must dry in a cool, dry and shady place such as the spare room until they are crisp to the touch and rustle like straw. Treated this way, once dried they are all ready to arrange. You can cover the wires with a stem tape if you wish. Crepe paper cut into narrow strips is ideal for this purpose but it is not usually necessary. Once arranged, the other perpetuelles should hide the wires quite effectively. The wires are matt, not shiny and so are inconspicuous in an arrangement.

If you do use tape begin applying it right up under the flower and then take it down the wire as you rotate it between finger and thumb in such a way that the tape spirals, covering the wire as it goes. Use a touch of adhesive to hold the end in place, both under the flower and at the base of the wire.

There are many other pretty little everlastings such as acrocliniums and rhodanthe but these are not often to be found on sale and you will have to grow them yourself. These can be left on their stems for they are quite tough as a rule. If their stems are not long enough for the arrangement in which they are to be used they can be mounted on florist's wires either singly or in small bunches.

Grasses and rushes

Also listed in seed catalogues are ornamental grasses. Every garden should have some of these for they really are beautifully decorative. Used in fresh flower arrangements they will often 'flower' in a way you might never see them bloom in a garden. The whole plume or inflorescence of the grass will be delicately hung with shimmering stamens. Those grasses which are used fresh in an arrangement can also be taken out and dried after use. However, the rule with these and also with any wild grasses you might gather is that the younger they are when picked the better colour they will be when dried. The time to pick all grasses, including the great cortaderia or pampas grass which blooms really late in the year, is just after the flowering part has emerged from its protective sheath.

Among the many grasses worth growing both for fresh and for dried arrangements are the quaking grass or briza, bromus or false oats, hare's tail and squirrel tail grasses and the farm cereals, oats, wheat and barley. (See also *The Flower Arranger's Garden*.)

There are many wild grasses well worth gathering. Most of these, enchanting when fresh and still lovely when dried, can be found quite easily once you know what you are looking for. Timothy grass resembles tiny green bulrushes and I find this grass extremely useful for bringing both height and contrast of shape to an arrangement. Incidentally, I always save the 'straws' cut from the ends of grasses which have to be shortened during arrangement, for these make splendid false stems. You can use them for all kinds of lightweight materials, such as individual leaves. Usually all that is needed to fix one to the other is a touch of adhesive.

Rushes of all kinds are useful to those who want to make really large decorations. Dry these and all grasses by hanging them in the way already described for flowers. Bulrushes, however, need special care. It is most important that these are gathered really young. If they are left to mature they will soon burst and spread their seed and be of no decorative value. You can tell a young bulrush because it is lighter in colour and still has part of the inflorescence on its tip like the wick of a candle. Cut the stems and stand the bulrushes in a heavy, tall vessel to dry. There is no special drying method and you can arrange them right away if you wish. Should you use them in water with fresh flowers, be sure to dry the stem ends after use.

Below: Among the hardy annuals which can be raised from seed for drying are helichrysum, rhodanthe, acroclinium and statice. Right: A dried arrangement can be built up as the materials come to hand. The tall fluffy 'clocks' are seeds of the pondside ligularia; top right, the seed cases of henbane; left, nicandra; centre, poppy, lotus and teasels.

Autumn is too late

So many people wait until the autumn before they begin to think about their winter dried flower arrangements. But by then it is much too late for so many things. One should begin making plans and harvesting early in the summer. Certainly many grasses should be gathered then, long before the haymaking begins. Those things that mature at the end of the summer should be cut before the frost touches them. All perpetuelles should be gathered on a dry day.

Many seed heads, poppies for example, can be cut when green, even used in fresh arrangements and then dried after use. The seed head should be fully developed and not far off the ripening stage. This is not to say that fully ripe fruits should not be cut. Often such things as empty seed pods of lily, yucca, bluebells, are perfect for arrangement, but there is always the danger that these may become damaged if left on the plant too long.

Many perpetuelles will last for years and can be used time and time again. If they become dusty they can be washed by swishing them around in water and detergent and then laying them out on newspaper in a warm, dry atmosphere to dry perfectly before being stored away again. A good way to store them is to hang them in plastic bags with the contents resting on their stems this time and not their heads.

Preserving in glycerine solution

One of the great stand-bys for an arranger is a plentiful supply of preserved foliage. While many people know that beech leaves cut in early autumn can be preserved in a solution of glycerine and water (one part glycerine and two parts boiling water), not all of them realise that many other leaves can be preserved by the same method. These can be leaves cut from garden shrubs, evergreen laurel, camellia, elaeagnus are splendid examples, or those bought from the florist such as eucalyptus, box, grevillea and pittosporum as well as a greaty variety of wild plant foliage. It really is worth while experimenting.

The stem ends need to stand only in 1–2 in. of the solution, so it is possible to preserve just one or two sprays of foliage at a time should this be most convenient. The one important thing is to make sure that the foliage will absorb the solution readily. It should first be stood for some hours in warmed plain water to harden. I like to let the branches stand overnight. You can soon tell if the water is moving through the veins. Curled or shrivelled leaves are a sign that the stems are not drinking and it would be pointless to try to make these take up the solution.

If they are stood in only a little of the glycerine solution spreading branches tend to be top heavy. It is best to pour a couple of inches into a narrow tin or jar and stand this inside a bucket or some heavier and larger vessel. The branches can then rest against the sides of the larger vessel.

It is not possible to say just how long a branch should stay in the solution. After a time you will notice a change in the leaves as the liquid travels up through the veins. In the case of eucalyptus, for example, the solution seems to travel very quickly and I have found it possible to remove the stems again in some 48 hours. The leaves retain their fine bluish green bloom yet they are preserved. If the eucalyptus is allowed to stand longer in the mixture the leaves turn dark, a little like copper beech. All the foliage turns colour. Evergreens such as laurel and camellia turn a lovely rich brown. Incidentally, all evergreens must be mature when treated. Young evergreen foliage will not absorb the solution.

The branches should not stand in the mixture so long that it exudes from the leaf surfaces, which it will do in some cases. I find that by the time all the solution has been taken up, using only about 2 in. in a 1 lb. jam jar, the leaves are normally preserved. One gets to know.

Mature ferns, that is those with their undersides well patterned with brown spores, can be treated in a similar fashion to the eucalyptus.

It is possible to preserve the fluffy seedheads of old man's beard or wild clematis by this method. The stems should be cut before the seed styles have begun to turn fluffy and are still green. You can preserve many green seed-heads such as gladioli, verbascum and iris and tall, striking foliage such as New Zealand flax.

Delphiniums and geraniums

Apart from these basic perpetuelles there are several fresh flowers which respond to drying, but unlike those already mentioned these must be dried quickly in a warm, dry place such as an airing cupboard or over a stove, though not in sunlight. Hang them upside down or else fit them right way up between the slats of the cupboard. Remove them only when they are quite dry to the touch.

These include such hardy perennials as delphiniums and their annual counterparts, larkspurs. Of these the pink and white varieties dry extremely well. The flat gold achillea, golden rod, hydrangeas and gypsophila are other examples. As with the foliage, it is well worth while experimenting. Some summers more things will dry than in other years. Sometimes one can dry zinnias, double sunflowers, marigolds and even double pelargoniums or pot geraniums quite easily. Late rosebuds frequently dry well.

Honesty moons are extremely attractive and blend well with so many other plant materials, although they can also look effective when used on their own. I like to gather these early in the season as soon as the flat seeds in the pods are mature. I pull up the entire plant and hang it upside down to dry in a cool, dry shed. From time to time I test it, then when I can easily pull the outer parts away from the shining central 'moon' I strip all the stems and bring them indoors for arrangement.

Physalis or Chinese lanterns are also extremely beautiful and long lasting. These mix well with preserved leaves that have turned a lovely leathery brown and with honesty, blue-green hydrangeas and wild clematis.

Cones, gourds and driftwood

Larch branches, so prettily studded with tiny nodules and flower-like cones are highly decorative, especially if you can find some which are smudged jade-green or grey with lichen. Larch can be used with individual larger cones of all kinds in a wooden mixture, the larch playing the role of the long stems defining the outline of the arrangement while the larger cones fill in the centre and act as blooms. The larch branches may need a little shaping and grooming. The cones will need mounting on false stems if they are to be handled effectively.

This is easily done if you use florist's wires. Place the wire against the cone about 1 in. above its base and pull it down among the scales so that it is hidden, leaving roughly equal portions of wire on each side. Bring these two ends around the cone, still down in between the scales, then bend them down below its base. This might make a stem of suitable length, but should you need a longer stem fasten the wire to a small cane or twig.

Cones look well with contrasting gleaming leathery brown leaves. Together they are good materials to arrange in heavy metal vessels or in deep brown glazed pottery. One texture complements the other. And speaking of cones, these do not have to be arranged in the strict sense of the word. They can

Left: This fascinating collection contains lotus seed pods, alligator pears, large seed pods from great trees and cones and gourds, all dried hard as wood. Below: Keep a table decoration of dried flowers ready for an occasion when there is no time to arrange fresh flowers. This one holds pink acroclinium and rhodanthe, rosy helichrysum and yellow and blue statice.

simply be piled on a dish. The secret lies in choosing the right container. One of my favourite decorations of this kind (and incidentally so long lasting that it is vacuum cleaned regularly!) is a scoop-shaped piece of modern Irish copper filled with a mixture of large seed pods and cases of all shapes, mostly from African trees but including also some dark brown lotus seed pods bought from the florist's sundriesman, two alligator pears now dried hard as wood, large cones and gourds. Visitors are fascinated by this little collection and they love to examine and even handle the contents.

Mixed gourds in a variety of shapes and colours look particularly rich and satisfying heaped in bowls about the house. For special occasions they can be arranged on a bed of leaves, with perhaps more foliage and even a few flowers such as dahlias, chrysanthemums, roses or carnations placed among them. Water-soaked blocks of OASIS wrapped in plastic or foil will hold the stems and keep them moist. These can be hidden by the fruit or foliage.

Driftwood fits in attractively with many arrangements of dried materials. It can be used as a base or to give height, width or even style. Or it can be merely used as a convenience and used to hide the mechanics of the composition. In this respect small pieces can be arranged to hide any small vessel or block of plastic which is holding the stems. Shells, pebbles, sea fans bought from a pet shop can also be introduced, just as they are in fresh flower arrangements.

Mixing fresh and dried

In some cases whole plants can be used. For instance the bromeliad cryptanthus, not unlike starfish in appearance, can be used as the focal point in a dried arrangement. These plants can be watered by spraying the foliage, should you find it difficult to reach the pots once these are arranged.

Fresh flowers can be mixed with dried ones and indeed you can achieve some very pleasant compositions this way. Make a good background of perpetuelles around an empty vase, preferably cone-shaped, pushed into the container near the rim. See that it can be lifted out and replaced easily. This can be kept filled with fresh blooms, berries or foliage. One successful arrangement I made like this was in a copper samovar. The outline was of pressed bracken, teasels and graceful seed heads. The fresh flowers were red anemones.

It is well worth while to make a table arrangement of dried flowers to store away. When you have unexpected guests and no time to arrange fresh flowers, an arrangement like this can be carefully slid from its clear plastic dust-sheet and used to greet and to cheer the visitors.

Making a dried arrangement

You will need to assemble a good quantity of materials. Flower for flower you will need more for a dried arrangement than for a fresh one.

Incidentally, if you are not bound by time and essential routine, it is a pleasant pastime to assemble these arrangements little by little as the materials come to hand, rather as you might paint a picture at weekends. This way you are most likely to get a delightful variety of materials and some highly individual arrangements.

But whatever method of assembly you adopt you must begin, of course, by selecting your containers. Remember that dried materials are light in weight and choose either heavy containers or weight them in some way. Gently pour some small gravel or some sand into the base of any vessel which is likely to tip over when filled. It is surprisingly easy to knock over a dried flower arrangement unless the container is weighted.

Perpetuelles look lovely in well-polished metals, but there usually comes a time when the metals need cleaning, not an easy matter sometimes when they hold a mass of flowers. Sometimes it is possible to lift out the arrangement without undue disturbance and to replace it in one piece after cleaning the container surfaces.

White vases and clear pastel colours are suitable for almost all dried materials. They seem to endow their contents with some of their own freshness. Usually gleaming textures look better than matt surfaces, for unfortunately these often pass on a dull effect to the dried flowers they hold.

To hold the stems I use OASIS and find that the very frail stems of grass and some dried flowers like rhodanthe need only be inserted a fraction of an inch into the plastic to be held quite firmly. And this again means that they need be handled only very lightly. Often if you have to push them down among many other stems into the wire netting you can bend or break the frail stems. The plastic block is used dry, of course. I find that arrangement is facilitated if the block projects a little way above rim level. You will then be able to push the side stems in quite easily.

Note: If you are interested in trying some more methods of drying foliage and flowers, these are described in another title in the Good Housekeeping Family Library, JAMS AND PRESERVES.

6 FLOWERS FOR SPECIAL OCCASIONS

Once you have grasped the fundamentals of flower arrangement you can apply them to all kinds of decorations. Often, for a wedding for instance, all that will be necessary will be for you to make arrangements wider, generally larger and possibly more lush than usual. Even then you can exercise your licence and introduce materials which are not strictly floral such as ribbons or baubles, or you can embellish simple materials to lift them from their everyday role. An example of this would be an arrangement of mixed flowers, white and soft pastel tints, backed by a framework of cycas leaves painted to match and glittered with Christmas frost. For similar purposes bleached shadow leaves mounted on branches can be margined with glitter. Should it be winter and flowers scarce or expensive there are quite a number of dried materials which can be given a sparkle in this way.

How to give them 'impact'

Large quantities of natural honesty can be used to blend with flowers. Bleached fern, grasses, foliage and seedheads will also look well. The important thing is to use plenty of fresh materials with them. If you are working to a low budget it is better to make several large arrangements like this and to give each an impressive centre of a few choice flowers than to rely on just one or two arrangements made entirely from fresh flowers.

Do bear in mind as you arrange them that you are looking at the flowers in comparative solitude. When they are on show there will be many people present. They really do have to be larger and fuller than usual if they are to make an impact.

Bear this in mind also when you decorate the tables. For a buffet one way of making sure that the flowers gain attention is to arrange them high. But if people are to sit at the tables at the same time you have to make sure that they do not obscure their view. Flowers can be raised in many ways by using water-retentive foamed plastic. One good way is to use champagne

Flowers for special occasions often need only to be a little more lush than usual. For an early summer wedding, the pastel tints of sweet peas, year-round chrysanthemums and forget-me-nots are a happy choice.

bottles filled with water to weight them as containers. Fit a piece of well-soaked plastic over the top of the neck of the bottle and arrange the flowers in this. You will find it quite easy to push the bottle neck up into the plastic.

If the reception is to be held in a marquee it may be possible to hang floral balls from the supports or on the sides of the tent. Use foamed plastic for these also in just the same way. Flowers to go on the ends of the pews in church can be arranged by this method also.

Flowering trees: Little trees of flowers can be made by fixing canes in a cellulose filler (such as POLYFILLA) in flower pots and topping them with OASIS balls. It is advisable to pour some shingle into the pots first to weight them and then to put the plaster on this. Wedge the canes upright in the shingle and pour on the plaster. Once the cane is set in position the plastic can be pushed on the top and flowers arranged in it. To prevent it slipping down the cane (it is heavy once soaked) twist a thick rubber ring around the cane where you wish the plastic to be held.

This is a useful style of decoration because you can adapt it to suit many purposes. For a party, for instance, you can make little lemon trees. First cover the foundation with snippets of evergreen to make it look like a little clipped round tree. Use plastic lemons which are light in weight to decorate it. Mount them on wires first.

You can play many variations on this theme. A rose tree in midwinter would not use many expensive flowers and on such an occasion you could even use paper flowers.

If you use a plastic cone shape (STYROFOAM) as a foundation you can carry the tree theme a little further. Christmas trees can be made this way. A pair of them look delightful on a buffet or on each side of a door. The foundation cones come in many sizes. You may not want to mount these on a long cane but instead have them sitting on the rim of the pot. All kinds of materials can be used to decorate these, many of them quite simple such as individual lanterns of physalis, large strawdaisies, glittered cones, glass baubles, or posies of rose hips or holly berries surrounded by a little collar of leaves.

Christmas decorations: The tree theme is a good one to carry in your mind when planning Christmas decorations. If you study a branch of spruce and most other conifers you will see that it is naturally triangular, a tree in two dimensions. Such a branch can be fixed to a piece of felt or a piece of board and then to a wall. It can be given a 'container' which consists merely of a flower pot cut out of felt or brown paper and then decorated. This is a good decorative theme where space is limited.

The same kind of branch, but smaller, can be used at the back of a Christmas flower arrangement. You can then arrange a few flowers before it, leaving the tree outline unbroken. Flowers can be complemented by any kind of seasonal material, including baubles as well as cones, berries and foliage of all kinds.

Flowers are not essential for Christmas arrangements. Those made entirely from foliage look well and they can be made extremely colourful by using all kinds of tree ornaments with them as well as fruit, seedheads and even

Snowflakes should always be based on six parts. The cycas leaves used here can be bought from a florist but well-shaped tips of spruce can be used in the same way.

ribbons. Whether or not you want them painted or glittered is a matter of personal taste.

Grasses can be lightly frosted, especially those kinds that hang prettily, such as bromus, because they will then become a little heavier and hang just a little lower. Incidentally, the easiest and least messy way of applying glitter is to put a little in a strong paper or plastic bag. Touch the material to be glittered very lightly with a little varnish or paint and then put it inside the bag and shake it up well, being careful to hold the top tightly closed. It is best to mount any materials that have false stems before doing this. You can then stand them in some vessel while they dry.

Frost and snowflakes: Paint and glitter need to be applied discreetly. Decorations are usually more effective if there is contrast between natural and glittered or painted materials. Sometimes it is more attractive to make a little frosting on a line down the midrib of large leaves or the centre of a branch, or around the margin of large leaves and the tips of side stems on a branch, even on the tips of cone scales, than it is to cover the whole area. The flat tree-on-a-wall described previously looks charming if a little artificial snow and frost are applied to the ends of the tips and if these also support a tree bauble. You can hang these on with black cotton or with fine wire.

Flat branches, usually those cut from the stem ends of larger branches, can be made into snowflakes, again by using a piece of plastic as a foundation. Slice a small cylinder of OASIS in half for this, or you might need a whole cylinder for a large arrangement. Select six (always six because a snowflake is six-pointed) equal lengths as uniform as possible and insert these around the outside of the cylinder at equal distances apart. Then arrange other different and shorter materials, again keeping to six, until you reach the very centre.

At Christmas there are a thousand variations that can be played on the 'tree' theme. One of the prettiest I ever made was this, composed of honesty hung with glass baubles.

This glowing little tree, composed of honesty, has an advantage over the traditional Christmas tree, in that it stays tidy and does not drop needles.

Finish this off with a bauble or a star, or even a white or yellow strawdaisy (see drawing on page 67).

Fir and candle table centres

These same flat branches of spruce or some other conifer can be used as foundations for table centres arranged either in or out of containers. One very simple method is to place them end to end, stem ends overlapping for about 2 in. Lash these stems together. On them tie one of the little rolls of plastic covered wire netting which are sold by stores for flower arrangement, or alternatively fix on a piece of plastic instead. Make sure that all stands firm. Insert a candle firmly so that it stands in the centre. If you are using wire netting don't worry if the candle does not immediately stand vertically and firmly. When you arrange materials around it their stems can be used to wedge it in place. Keep these materials low so that the candle stands well above them. The candle is really used for colour and atmosphere and is not intended to be lit. If you do wish to light the candles in such arrangements, see that really tall ones are used or that any shorter ones are raised. You can lash them to thin canes, one on each side.

Having made this basic start from two stems you can then add anything you wish, following the rules for making an all-round arrangement (see page 16), with the candle as the centre stem. As you arrange all the stems point their ends towards the base of the candle and let each one rise a little further from the flat foundation stems.

These first two stems can if you wish be lashed to a small mat to ensure that they will not scratch a table top or other piece of furniture. Or you can begin by arranging them in the manner of any flower arrangement by using a container. There are many shallow expendables that will do for this, such as the plastic trays in which mushrooms are packed for retail sale. If you want the table decoration to last fresh for as long as possible then it is best to use well-soaked OASIS inside a waterproof container of some kind.

Strip the stem ends and slant the cuts for easy arrangement. You can often use the little laterals which are stripped off. If these are small, like fern fronds for instance, make five or more into a fan. Wire these by mounting them on florist's wire and use them as clusters. Really small snippets of bright leaves such as variegated holly, elaeagnus or golden privet are all that are necessary if you are trying to make a little go a long way. If you have the time and patience you can arrange them around a little cluster of berries.

Extending a stem: Sometimes it is difficult to arrange individual leaves because their stems are so short. You can ease this situation by extending the stem. Insert something such as a cocktail stick or a portion of florist's wire up the short stem, leaving enough protruding to go easily into the arrangement. If the leaves have to be in water it will be enough for the last fraction of an inch of the stem to be moist, so do not attempt to push the leaf in as far as its blade.

Cocktail sticks can be used quite often for all kinds of materials and in many types of arrangement. Individual leaves cut from the beautiful

Above: Swags of this type are easily made on a foundation of rolled newspaper, old stocking or a length of fabric. The evergreen snippets are bound on first. Berries, fruits, cones and other decorations are mounted on false stems and added afterwards. Right: Pine cones of all kinds can be used in swags or ropes. They should first be mounted on wires or pipe-cleaners. Small cones and little sprigs of berried holly, also mounted, are arranged between the large cones. Dried maple and skeleton lime leaves make a pretty topknot.

Left: A Christmas party garland made from a windfallen branch of monkey puzzle tree. Pieces cut from the end were sliced through to make 'flowers'. The ends of the branch were wired together and concealed under the decorations, and the garland was then sprayed with gold. Above: The cabbage hides the container holding the candles and anemone-centred chrysanthemums. Most of the components are held on a shallow tray.

ornamental kale, for example, are seldom quite long enough to let you arrange them at whatever angle appeals to you. The stick in the stem gives you just an inch or two more, which makes all the difference. I use them also to give apples and other fruits a good stem and for adding the final decorations to garlands, swags and other kinds of Christmas decorations; materials such as tiny crab apples, physalis lanterns, tangerines, helichrysums, beech nut clusters and cones.

A swag for the front door

Garlands and ropes are really quite easy to make, but you need to allow yourself plenty of time both to gather the considerable quantity of materials required and to cut these into small snippets. However, you can make a welcome swag for the front door quite quickly, again using two flat conifer branches. Lash these together but not quite so formally this time, for both ends need not be equal nor their tips opposite. Aim for a crescent shape. Arrange them so that the tips of both arch downwards. Fix something behind them so that you will be able to hang the swag nicely and test it for balance.

Next, fix a piece of wire netting or a piece of plastic over the tie in the manner described for the table centre, although you are not likely to want such a large piece of wire netting. Again, arrange the other materials as though you were filling a bowl, but remember that it will ultimately hang on its side. Don't make it too regular and formal. Bells made from cream cartons and covered with foil, baubles of all kinds (use unbreakable ones if the arrangement is to hang out of doors) and glittered cones can hang in festoons from the centre. If it is for indoors you can arrange a bow at the back of the foundation branches. Give it several loops and see that these are long enough to show beyond the greens. The tails of the bow also should show; they should be cut on a slant, not fish-tail fashion. Customarily, ribbons are cut this way only for funerals.

Making garlands and ropes

You can make garlands on various kinds of foundations including wire coat hangers pulled into a ring shape. The only thing is that these are fairly small. A strong wire hoop is better and it is easier to attach evergreens to it if it is first covered. Use tapes made by cutting through folded crepe paper. Swags or ropes (see drawings on page 71) can be made on foundations of such things as old nylon stockings or rolled newspapers.

Have ready short pieces of evergreens cut into 4–6 in. lengths. These have to be tied on to the foundation. For ropes it is best to begin at the tips and work towards the centre and to do a little of each end as you go; otherwise the result will almost certainly be uneven. When you arrive at the centre make a separate little spray and attach this so that the stem ends are hidden. If you intend to hang a swag over a mantelpiece, doorway or mirror, with ropes coming down on each side, it is best to make separate lengths and to hang them to cover the joints in such a way that they look like one continuous length.

To bind the evergreens use either green garden twine or florist's reel wire. When you bind them lay one piece in place, pass the binding material over the stem and pull tight. Lay the next piece on this so that it covers the binding of the previous piece with its tip 1–2 in. below that of the first to be tied. Continue this way. Always try to pass the binding between leaves and stem instead of taking it over a leaf and so disfiguring its shape. Not only will it look better this way, it will stay firm. Stems are not so likely to shrink as leaves.

You can see that the sprigs of green need to be fairly substantial though short. If you try to use long pieces it will not be possible to keep the outline neat and compact. If the evergreens are not bushy, bunch two or three pieces together, but you will find that one piece is easiest to use. Mixed evergreens are pretty but you need to have them much the same size, like box and yew for example. You can use pieces of larger-leaved evergreens for decoration after the basic framework has been completed.

When you make a garland work all around it in one direction and when you reach the starting point again neaten the area this way. Take a substantial though not long piece of evergreen and lay it with its tip pointing inwards and upwards. Bind it in place and lay another piece pointing in the opposite direction. At this point, and with these two pieces as foundation, arrange the decorations. Whether you use cocktail sticks or florist's wire to mount the decorations, see that they follow the line of whatever design you have made.

HARVEST ARRANGEMENTS

Any kind of occasion in autumn provides an excuse to give decorations a harvest touch. Flowers and fruit look so well together. At one time much ingenuity had to be employed to get an apple or whatever to stay just as you wanted it, but now usually all you have to do is push it firmly into a piece of foamed plastic. You may find that it is best to arrange the fruit first. It is always simpler to push a stem away out of sight and to curve a flower around than it is to lower several fruits down into the centre of a group of flowers so that they look attractive and at ease.

If the arrangement is only intended to last a little while there is no harm

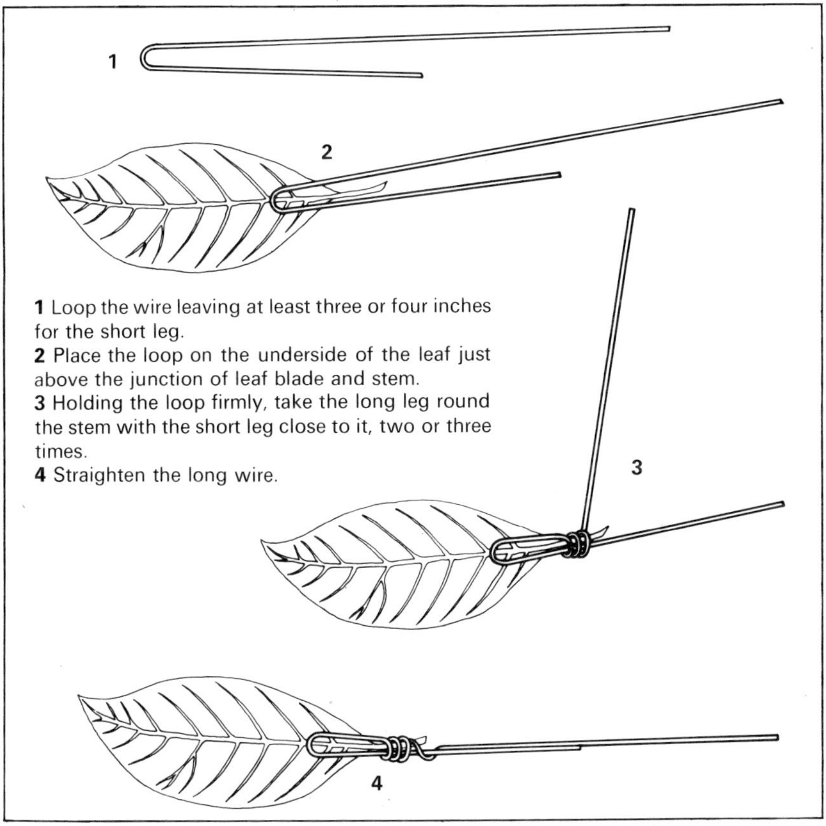

1 Loop the wire leaving at least three or four inches for the short leg.
2 Place the loop on the underside of the leaf just above the junction of leaf blade and stem.
3 Holding the loop firmly, take the long leg round the stem with the short leg close to it, two or three times.
4 Straighten the long wire.

in the fruit being in contact with moisture, and when this is the case the same block of plastic which supports one can succour the other. Often you will need to arrange the fruit and maybe even the flowers and foliage on different planes. You can elevate them by using blocks of OASIS, although these need not be very thick. One can be anchored to another quite firmly by pushing a cane, twig or cocktail stick down through one to the other. Any joins and subterfuges of this nature can be hidden by the flowers.

Much depends upon the nature of the arrangement and sometimes the fruits have to be positioned after arranging the flowers. Various means can be used to lift and support them. Sometimes individuals, an apple or a gourd turned so that its attractive centre is facing forward, can be held and properly displayed in a circular object such as a napkin ring. Pastry cutters are also good for this purpose. The support can be hidden by a leaf or by some other similar means. At other times I have used a piece of clean, dry bark or cork laid across the rim of the container. Often fruits are mounted and arranged separately like the flowers.

Florist's wires and even pipe cleaners are useful sometimes for the actual stem, in which case they have to be long enough to pass two or three times round the stem of the subject being arranged and then go down deep into the container. However, these are sometimes just not heavy enough to anchor themselves properly and this is particularly the case when a large bunch of grapes is being arranged. A length of cane can come to your aid here or some stout twig. The bunch can be tied, wired or taped to this. Just bear in mind that the weightier the material to be mounted the more rigid must be the false stem which supports it.

Making a 'double leg': So much depends upon whether or not the fruit being used has a stem or leaf-stalk. Where this exists, even if it is quite short it is sometimes possible to splice a false stem onto it. But often this little stem becomes detached after arrangement. Because of this the whole fruit has to be wired instead by passing a wire through it from one side to the other. It is best to do this in such a way that the wire is not conspicuous. As a rule you can pass it through quite well some little way above its natural stem area. The method is to leave roughly equal lengths of wire protruding on each side. These are then known as 'double legs' or 'double mounts'. The wires are then brought down as close as possible to the surface of the fruit and then twisted together directly below it, again as close to the surface as possible. Sometimes these two wires together will be firm enough to act as a stem, but should this not be the case they can be twisted around a cane or taped to it. Adjust the angle at which you want the fruit to be displayed before inserting the stem and make any other small adjustments after it is in position.

Quite often, and especially if the arrangement is not expected to last for a long time, it is possible to insert the wires or even a thin stiff cane into the base of the fruit, roughly at the point where its stem should be. If the fruit is heavy you may need to treat two or more wires held close together as a single wire. Cocktail sticks can be used for this purpose in arrangements where only short stems are necessary. Sometimes you can insert the wire or the cane up through the centre of a short petiole, like that of an artichoke for instance. If you use thick wires for this instead of canes you will be able to bend them to make the fruit face your required direction after it has been mounted. The 'double leg' technique is used in floristry for various other purposes such as mounting leaves; see diagrams on page 75.

Fruit and vegetables

There are many beautiful vegetables for the flower arranger to choose from; many of them, though by no means all, are botanically speaking 'fruits', but whichever their classification, they are certainly decorative enough to be used.

An Easter arrangement of early double tulips and Roman hyacinths, both sweetly scented and both easy to grow indoors. With them are a few early crocuses and hazel catkins.

1

2

Left: **1** A basket is lined with plastic and block or crumbled foamed plastic stem-holder. This is thoroughly soaked and placed over wire netting to provide the moisture. Moss for the nest covers one half. **2** The tallest catkin stems and other twigs are arranged first with a few flowers to set the style. The eggs are then laid on the moss. If necessary, a small piece of plastic can be placed under them to protect them from the moisture.

Mushrooms can look most attractive in certain situations. They can be displayed the right way up or turned so that their pretty undersides are on view. A cocktail stick inserted in the fleshy centre of the tops of those which are to show their undersides, or in the stem bases of others, will enable you to arrange them quite easily.

Sweet corn is so heavy that it can be difficult to arrange, which is a pity because in large arrangements it can be so effective. I use strong, long florist's wires and pull them tightly around the stem of the cob to make a double leg mount. This is then fixed to a cane and the best way to do this is to lay one of the wires close to the cane, holding it there while the other leg is passed around, binding its fellow to the cane at the same time. Finally as an extra precaution I use a little transparent sticky tape at the top of the cane to fix all firmly in place. After mounting the corn this way the cob can be gently moved to assume the required position or angle as you exert pressure at the point where the wires were twisted around.

You can make some really effective large arrangements by using the cobs as flowers. To do this cut the outer sheath so that you can turn the tissues back to resemble petals with the cob as the flower's centre. In arrangements of this type the outsize pampas grass can be used. Other suitable components on the same scale are the deep brown lotus seed heads which can be bought from specialist shops. Artichokes and cardoons are also effective.

Decorating large areas

Rhododendron foliage can be turned into 'poinsettias' by painting the tips of the branches a bright scarlet, a coral pink or a greenish-white, the colours of poinsettias, although the red varieties are best known.

Cycas leaves bought from the florist's sundriesman can also be used to cover large areas. They come in several sizes. For large arrangements some may have to be mounted on thin canes. You can save considerable time and trouble if you mount them on a strong wire near the base (the clear portion of stem is very short) and then fix three or five fan-wise to a cane. This way you need only arrange one stem. This is a good method to use when vases have fairly small apertures, such as those of some church vases for example. You can buy bleached cycas which can be sprayed or glittered. The green fronds are rather dark and heavy and may need tinting.

Another means of quickly decorating a large area—either on a wall or the apron of a buffet table—is to use swags or ropes of leaves and flowers as described earlier. The simplest method of all is simply to take trails of ivy and loop them, making a special knot of leaves, flowers, fruit, even doyleys at the junction of one loop with the next.

Swags can be made of things other than winter evergreens. Pressed bracken and other ferns come to mind and helichrysums and other dried flowers can be used, but not, I would advise, on a buffet apron in case someone drops a cigarette end on them. Reserve these for wall decorations.

Heaps and cones of fruits, flowers and vegetables are always effective. These too can be made some time ahead of the event.

Easter arrangements

Eggs always seem to be featured in one way or another in Easter arrangements. The thing to do is to decide what flowers and leaves you are likely to use and then to colour the eggs to harmonise with them. Little arrangements of this nature make charming gifts, especially for people who live in towns.

You need not limit yourself to whole or fresh eggs; the shells of your breakfast boiled eggs can be used, if arranged carefully, so that the broken ends are hidden. These can also be arranged by being placed on top of drinking straws to act as stems. Eggs, bleached barley or wheat and oats will blend remarkably effectively with primroses, daisies and daffodils. Naturally enough, catkins, blossom and fresh young leaves with flowers and eggs and even toy chicks are both pretty and popular, especially with the young.

Easter arrangements give you an opportunity to use small bunches of flowers, either from the garden or little wild ones that the children bring home. Make each into a tiny posy surrounded by a collar of leaves, ivy leaves for instance. You can arrange these little posies in many ways, for example in a simple circle around the rim of a deep plate with a pile of eggs, lifted from the water by placing the plate which holds them on a small jar or napkin ring. You can arrange them in a cone by building up a series of plates and saucers, each one lifted from the other on an eggcup or something similar. Make quite sure that all stands firmly before you begin the arrangement. Arrange the posies on the plates, their stems to the centre. Lay them on crumbled OASIS. If you use a pencil or something similar to make holes for the stem ends you can follow the tree pattern or perhaps a Byzantine cone (see diagram on page 15) and make one of all posies.

Containers for special occasions

It is important to choose the right containers for special flowers. At times when flowers are scarce a coloured container can do much to add to the general effect, but make a discreet choice. Make sure that the container does not dominate the flowers.

When you are making a special arrangement for a dinner or luncheon party you might be able to take part of the china you intend using and make your arrangement in this. Quite often vegetable or soup tureens will not be needed for the food and they make excellent flower bowls. You can strike a pleasant harmony this way. Failing the actual tureen, use an anonymous container for the flowers, say a plain white bowl, and stand this on a plate from the service so that the pattern shows and is actually a part of the arrangement. It goes without saying that the flowers, china and linen should harmonise. In this respect these others can help you. For instance if you make an arrangement of mainly foliage and introduce just a few flowers into it, see that your candles and napkins match them. You can give the impression of using many more flowers than is actually the case, a useful tip if you have to buy them in times of scarcity.

You can let your imagination run riot at Christmas time and use anything that seems in keeping with the mood of the moment. It is surprising how well junk vessels look once they have evergreens and berries in them, strange ornate urns, chalices, tankards, steins and things of this nature.

Rustic or elegant: Logs can be scooped out and filled with a food tin just large enough for a cylinder of OASIS. False logs can be made from bark or cork curled around tins or perhaps a block of OASIS wrapped in foil if it is to be used with water. Candlesticks and candle cups are 'naturals' at this season as are candles themselves. Goblets of coloured glass look well, especially when baubles are used in place of flowers and these opaque or semi-opaque vessels hide any stem-holder you might have to use. If you have only clear glass goblets consider first lining them with cooking foil. Put the stem-holder inside this. You can make a good 'silver' vase this way.

Trays of polished metal or wood make good base-containers especially for arrangements on side tables. A small supplementary container can hold the water, stem-holders and flowers; the other materials can be arranged on the tray itself.

For Easter arrangements where eggs and possibly chicks are to be used the accent needs to be on the rustic look. Baskets and wickerwork look well with flowers. There are enough shapes in these materials to give one a really wide choice.

Balance scales, metal scoops, wooden measures and various polished boxes suit fruit and flowers and bring a pleasant atmosphere. Place mats made from rush, split cane or coarsely woven linen can be used like the trays as base-containers. They can provide attractive contrasts in textures.

Finally, when planning arrangements for special occasions, consider using cut flowers or foliage and plants together. If you can use a striking pot-plant or two as the main portion of an arrangement you can cover a great deal of ground at one stroke. For parties the accompanying material can be on a vaster scale than you would normally use. For instance, whole branches of silver birch, themselves like tiny trees, can tower above a group of plants lower down. This method of arrangement, known as *pot-et-fleur*, is described in the *Flowers You Buy* chapter.

7 THE FLOWER ARRANGER'S GARDEN

If I had a tiny garden and had to choose what to grow that would help me most in flower arrangement I would grow foliage plants first and then make what space I could for flowers for cutting. The reason for this is that it is always possible to buy some cheap flowers but the kinds of leaves you can buy are limited. More than this, you can make delightful arrangements the year through by using leaves with the occasional branch of blossom, seed heads, fruits and grasses, but it is not so easy to maintain a consistent standard of charming and original arrangements by using flowers alone.

If you have a large garden you have no problem so far as a continual supply of materials is concerned. But even so, you should grow as much foliage for cutting as possible. It is interesting that since flower arrangement became so popular in this country the sale of plants such as hostas, bergenias, Solomon's seal, alchemilla have increased and also that almost every flower arranger with a garden now has a selection of 'green' flowers. 'They are so kind to other flowers', one told me.

Fortunately as far as some species are concerned these plants are not only handsome furnishings for both house and garden but have other values too. Some are good ground covers, others grow well in the shade. They need no staking. So first a review of foliage plants.

Silver and grey foliage

There are many grey or silver plants which are delightful for use with soft pastel tints and ideal for all foliage arrangements. One word of warning: some of these are very downy and if the stem portion is not properly stripped it will act as a wick when in water and cause a siphon. So when you strip the leaves from the portion to go under water, take some also from the portion above the rim for at least 1 in. Another tip. Some of these plants, ballota for example, are reluctant to take water when cut. However, if you avoid picking only the young growth and take a little of the old wood as well you should encounter no difficulty. Split the hard stem end and harden the piece in the usual way.

Many of these silver plants dry well and with little trouble. Some of those which grow in rosettes, such as verbascum, can be dried whole. Otherwise leaves can be pressed and here the downy kinds need to be brushed lightly to fluff them out again and eliminate the flatness when they are arranged.

Artichokes and cardoons can be grown in large gardens and these provide great leaves and giant flowers for those who are likely to wish to make large scale decorations.

There are also artemisias, santolinas, phlomis, senecios, olearias, anaphalis, helichrysum and many others. Of them all I use *Centaurea candidissima* and *Cineraria maritima* the most, pressing the largest leaves for dried arrangements. Seedsmen sometimes offer varieties of these 'Dusty Millers' and they are easily grown from seed. Most silver plants are also easily raised from cuttings.

Incidentally, one of the pleasant things about these plants is that they are evergreens—or greys. Some cannot tolerate our long wet winters and most do better in a sheltered place. However, I have little time to fuss over my own plants and my own silver border is always well furnished, even in mid-winter. Some plants can be lifted and potted in winter. A cloche will protect others. Give them really well-drained soil.

Cabbage 'roses'

Variegated plants produce striking leaves which bring light and interest into arrangements. It is always possible also to match some flower with the hues in the leaf, which means that you can make attractive arrangements from very simple flowers.

Examples that come to mind instantly are the ornamental cabbage and kale. The kale is left to seed itself in my own garden but it is usually most convenient to sow it fresh each year. The leaves are at their most beautiful during winter and early spring. At this time when flowers are scarce a few leaves of vivid magenta or some of soft cream and jade green are extremely welcome. The 'flower' cabbage can, like the kale, be grown in exactly the same way as the vegetable and you can also make several sowings of cabbage to prolong the season. I find it most useful in late autumn and winter.

If you care to sow a row of seed thinly and to let it grow unthinned you can raise a whole crop of tiny cabbage 'roses' which can act as flowers in arrangements. Whether or not you cut off the root is up to you, but if you leave it on you can replant the cabbage, deeper than it was before, and it will recover enough for you to be able to use it again another day.

Do not hesitate to use ordinary cabbages as 'roses'. Sometimes the leaves are prettily coloured. The red pickling cabbages look particularly good in arrangements. I like to pretend that these are outsize flowers and I use them at the foot of early forced spring blossom and catkins. Once again, if you want these for flower arrangement sow a row and let it grow unthinned. Green cabbage can be lightly glittered and used in Christmas arrangements. Brussels sprouts, broccoli and all brassica leaves turn handsome colours at times and all of them can be used individually with flowers.

The twirling hosta: Hostas are remarkable among shade plants in that they will tolerate drips from dense foliage overhead. These are lovely peren-

Globular leek seed heads, glaucous poppy capsules and leaves, lupin seed pods, honesty moons and columbine leaves make a flowerless yet pleasing arrangement.

nials and the leaves last a long time when cut. The foliage differs according to the species. The variegated forms are most highly valued and these differ also in subtle ways. It is best to go to a garden centre or nursery and choose which variegations appeal to you most. There is a lovely white margined hosta, *albo-marginata*. Similar is *H. undulata*. The twirl into which the leaves sometimes grow is due to the waved margins and arrangements made from these are strangely appealing. The individual leaves of this particular species are very large and will grow up to two feet or more from lobe to apex. However, most hostas are small and neat enough for the average size arrangement. Besides the variegated kinds there are hostas which have beautiful leaves with a bluish-green bloom. They have attractive flowers, spires of lavender, lily-like bells.

After the leaves have faded they remain on the plant until they are sapped of green matter and look bleached. If you gather them just before they begin to curl and steep them in old rain water they will become 'skeletonised'.

Brilliantly coloured leaves

There are many attractive foliage plants among annuals and bedding plants.

Ornamental kale in purple and jade (and also in cream, white and green) is easy to grow from seed. Cabbage flowers, nasturtiums, pansies, dianthus and stems of tomatoes look well in a copper jelly mould.

Many varieties of pelargoniums or pot geraniums for instance have beautifully coloured leaves. One variety with red flowers and golden foliage marked with bronze is Mrs Pollock. Almost as vividly marked as a parrot tulip is Henry Cox, which has gold, silver and bronze with red. There are others, some green and white.

Atriplex or mountain spinach has varieties with red foliage called *atrosanguinea, cupreata* and *rosea*. Sow the seeds from March onwards in succession if you want a continual supply. I like perilla, a half-hardy annual which has dark, fringed, copper beech purple foliage. The old fashioned clary has topknots coloured purple, rose, magenta or indigo, which are not strictly leaves but bracts. The plants are easy to grow, dainty and long-lasting when cut. One of the spurges, *Euphorbia marginata,* is an extremely handsome half-hardy annual, a little difficult to raise unless you have a greenhouse but well worth growing. Another euphorbia is known as annual poinsettia. This is the Mexican fire flower, *E. heterophylla*.

Many of the euphorbias or spurges are green. Botanically the flowers are most interesting. They are really a wonderful combination (like the poinsettia) of leaves, bracts and flowers, mainly green. But what greens! Some become coloured bright yellow, orange or deep wine at times according to their species.

All of them have a milky sap, the flow of which must be checked immediately the stems are cut.

Outstanding among them is *Euphorbia epithymoides* which flowers in April and is so bright that it shines out in any garden. The flowers are a sharp green yellow at first. By May the flower colour changes to a delicate pale green and the plant continues to decorate the border, and like all spurges changes slightly from month to month until the autumn. As it matures (and this also is the case with all spurges) it appears to take water a little better and lasts longer. There are many others, including the native wood spurge and I would not like to be without them. *E. pilosa major* has vivid yellow flowers and it takes on the loveliest colours in the autumn, ruby, crimson and bronze made from the fusing of the reds and greens. It is a good ground cover, too good sometimes, so I pull up the stems I wish to use. Alchemilla is another yellow-green flower. The foamy clusters of flowers can be dried and the lobed leaves are particularly lovely. It will grow in quite ordinary soil but it likes a well-drained site.

The green-flowered hellebore

Hellebores are valuable because they bloom at a time when bulb flowers dominate the scene and so they offer one a different shape, a different texture and atmosphere. Apart from the well-known white Christmas rose there are many others, most of them green-flowered. The loveliest of these is probably the Corsican type, *Helleborus viridis*, or the evergreen hellebore, which grows up to 1½ ft. and blooms in March. The flowers persist a long time. There are other species, all handsome. Most hellebores grow naturally in the cool, damp shade of woods. They will grow in an east border which is useful, but the soil must never be sodden nor likely to become waterlogged.

Ready to seed freely and to produce delightful and subtle differences in its offsprings' flowers is the Lenten rose, *H. orientalis*. The stems will grow as high as 2 ft. The species is rose pink but there are several varieties nowadays, mainly purple and green mixtures. It grows well on limestone soils.

Another flower which has come gradually to the forefront thanks to the hybridist is bergenia, also known as saxifrage or megasea. This plant will grow in the poorest of soils and in any situation, although it prefers a moist spot where it will grow into huge and most decorative clumps. The flowers come early in the year and although these are beautiful it is the leaves which are of such great value to flower arrangers. These are evergreen except in the bleakest of winters or the coldest of gardens. In the autumn they turn a most splendid crimson. New varieties differ in their leaf coloration as well as in their flowers.

Shrubs and trees

Many shrubs produce suitable foliage for cutting and I have already mentioned two with silver-backed leaves, senecio and olearia; these grow well in coastal areas. In both these genera you will find many species to choose from, if you visit a good garden centre or nursery.

Do remember when you plant shrubs with a view to cutting them for flower arrangement that they must be given a chance to establish themselves before they are robbed. Once this time has passed the shrubs will need attention. Weak wood, crossing or rubbing branches, misshapen pieces and traces of damage or disease will need to be cut away. If you do this when you are gathering materials for your flower arrangements you can do two jobs at the same time.

Pussy willow should really be reserved for a large garden and should never be planted near a building. *Salix daphnoides* produces lovely catkins which have a slight purple tinge while they are still in the 'kitten' stage. Those who enjoy making stylised arrangements will like the fasciated willow Setsuka, with twisted, flattened growths.

Another catkin tree, not so well known but much more acceptable for a small garden—since it can, and indeed should, be planted against a warm west or south wall if no other protected site can be found—is the evergreen *Garrya elliptica*. Its grey-green tassels, some tints lighter than the leaves, are both elegant and freely produced. Elaeagnus is a lovely evergreen which comes in greys and variegated forms. Flower arrangers like it not only for its long-lasting golden and other brightly coloured leaves but also because these will take a glycerine solution well and perform well as a dried material. The result is nothing like the fresh foliage. The leaves turn to various tans, extremely pleasing and with the texture of soft leather.

Blossom for forcing plays an important part in the flower arranger's garden. The flowering currants, both the well-known pink or American kind and the sweet-smelling yellow or Buffalo currant will take little room. And of course if you do cut them freely you will be able to keep them well under control. You can cut any branch of any shrub or tree for forcing indoors once the shortest day has passed.

Growing flowers for cutting

Even if you like masses of flowers indoors you will not want to rob the garden of so many that it loses its appeal and its colour. It is a sad fact that flowers last nothing like so long when they are cut as they do on the living plant. Take daffodils for instance, which will last six weeks on the bulb yet even when you cut them in bud the longest you can hope to have them looking decorative is about ten days. So it is an advantage, if you have the room, to grow a few rows of flowers, such as sweet peas, just for cutting. The modern varieties give long stems carrying many flowers, and if left to grow naturally up twiggy sticks or wire netting, develop tendrils and attractive side stems. They produce so many of these that they can be cut to complement the flowers.

The netting which supports my peas forms one side of a vast cage under which is my vegetable garden, so in fact no great space is given up to them. You can grow a row of peas like this as a screen, a division between one part of the garden and another, or along one side of a patio or sitting-out area. Alternatively, an extremely decorative and practical way of

Left: Green wood spurge is surrounded by maple leaves, golden privet and the round centres of faded doronicum daisies. Behind them are tall stems of tellima and grasses. Below: Roses harmonise with all kinds of other flowers. Old moss roses, modern floribundas, and shrub rugosa are blended with a rich assortment of garden flowers.

growing them is to make tripods of canes and twiggy sticks and station them in a mixed border.

There are so many annuals, both hardy and half-hardy, that every flower arranger can find plenty to suit both taste and need. Even those in borders can be cut without great loss, for as a rule the more you cut these plants the more they grow. Annuals for cutting are easily cared for if they are grown in rows. As they grow you can fix a string along each side to keep them upright if you have no twiggy sticks to support them. Alternatively you can use very large mesh wire netting, chicken wire. Fold this tent-wise, place it over the rows and the plants will grow up through it. Other netting, including that sold as pea netting, can be stretched over the rows.

If you sow hardy annuals in September you will get flowers earlier the following year than if you sowed them in the spring. If you have cloches to spare you can protect them and get them earlier still. Actually I prefer to use my cloches to put over rows of polyanthus, anemones, wallflowers and other spring flowers. This means that not only are they brought into flower earlier but that the flowers themselves are beautifully clean and unweathered. Hellebores, Christmas roses in particular, are much better when covered this way.

Anemones and irises

Anemone coronaria grows in a row in my garden, along the edge of a path with a row of calendulas behind them and gladioli behind these, all in less than 3 ft. of width. Anemones are so easy to grow. Of the two types sold for cutting, St. Brigid are the semi-double pastel hues and Du Caen, sometimes called poppy anemones, are in various bright colours and are single. They like a warm situation and a rich leaf-mould soil. It is as well to feed the soil or border in preparation for them. These flowers do not like a peaty, acid soil, so if there is a tendency in this direction it should be corrected by adding lime. Although many sizes of corms are offered I find that one gets extremely good results from small corms, 2–3 or 2–4 cm.

It is unwise to pick anemones which are too tight in bud in cold weather, if they are not covered by cloches. They seem to get frosted within themselves and consequently never expand properly. It is much better to cover them so that they can mature naturally. Pick them in bud, but only when the petals' colours are well defined. Many more flowers than most people realise can be cut in bud. Almost all those which grow from bulbs will continue to open in water. Irises are best cut in bud, particularly if they are to be transported; they do not get damaged this way.

Bulbous irises are just the things to grow in a row. If you care to leave the row they will come up year after year. These are Spanish irises, derived from *I. xiphium,* and their range grows every year. There are some lovely colours among them. If you plant them at fortnightly intervals you can have a succession of flowers to cut. The same applies to gladioli. Many short rows for both these flowers planted at intervals serve you better than one long one with everything in it planted at the same time.

Ornamental grasses

Once you have grown a few ornamental grasses you are likely to want always to have a few plants in the garden. They really can be quite beautiful when seen at close quarters. Used fresh and in their prime they blend beautifully with many kinds of flowers. It is a revelation to discover the violet, rose, carmine and blue of their inflorescences, colours one had never suspected were dusted over the grasses.

Seedsmen sell both collections and mixtures of ornamental grasses. Some of those worth growing are *Aira capillaris*; meadow foxtail or *A. pratensis* and *Briza minor* and *B. maxima,* both quaking grasses. You may have found wild examples growing. Sometimes *B. minor* is called the pearl grass because of the soft pearly texture of the inflorescence. Perhaps a little more difficult to grow than the others (it is best to treat it like sweetcorn, which it resembles), is *Coix lacryma-jobi,* or Job's tears. This is a striking plant in appearance; each heart-shaped 'tear' hangs gracefully from a tiny stem. There is also a variegated form. These grasses will dry but when used in their fresh state they are truly beautiful and unusual.

Stipa pennata is a long feathery grass which was once used a lot in table decorations when it was the fashion to 'add something light'. I find that it is best to strip the 'feathers' of leaves and then to bunch several together treated as one stem. Although you may have seen hare's tail grasses dried—these soft, fluffy things are very popular—they are simply delightful and quite different when used fresh. Gradually the grass matures in the vase and one day each fluffy head is smothered with tiny swinging stamens of palest golden yellow. Another lovely 'animal' grass is *Hordeum jubatum,* or squirrel tail grass. The long brushes are silky and fine. If you gather any of these grasses for drying only, be sure to pick them young, soon after the plume has emerged from its protective sheath.

Native plants and herbs

Surprisingly perhaps, many of the most popular materials for cutting, such as alchemilla, are native plants. Of recent years the wild arum has been found a place in many a strange suburban plot; this is the 'lords and ladies' of the hedgerows. *Arum maculatum* has spotted leaves, arrow shaped and very handsome. The leaves are favoured more highly than the flowers, but I like these strange green blooms. However, even if the flowers do not appeal to you don't disdain the leaves. The plant will grow quite happily beneath some shrub. I have one that lives at the foot of a shrub rose and another grows under a sumach.

Angelica produces almost globular umbels or flower-clusters which are extremely useful and handsome in large arrangements. The flowers vary in tone according to their maturity, being sometimes green, rose or greeny-white. *Angelica archangelica* is the herb used for flavouring liqueurs and its stems are candied for confectionery. It grows up to 5 ft. There is a smaller, 4 ft. species, *A. sylvestris,* with white flowers. Both of these plants like a shady place with deep, moist loam.

Many culinary and other herbs can be used for flower arrangement. The lovely blue-green rue can be gathered the year round. So too can the purple-leaved sage, lavender and rosemary. The perennial fennel has umbels of yellow flowers which look well in autumnal arrangements and of course any of the umbels can be dried and used in winter arrangements. They are very effective when frosted and used in Christmas decorations.

Robbing the rose garden

Of all the flowers in the garden, roses are the most frequently picked for flower arranging. Modern varieties of roses flower so freely and over so long a period that you can gather many flowers without robbing, spoiling the appearance of the bush, or taking colour from the garden. There is no need ever to take the cluster of floribunda roses; those individuals that make up the group have stems long enough for you to fit them into some arrangement or other. If you go over the bushes as if you were stealing the blooms and wanted no one to discover your crime you can find a surprising number!

At the end of the season, especially if we have a mild autumn, the bushes go on and on producing buds. Cut these before they become weathered. Watch over them and as soon as you see the calyx bending back away from the petals cut the stem. These already moving buds will continue to grow in water and will slowly develop into full blown roses.

8 FLOWERS YOU BUY

Those who have to buy all their flowers will find that flower arrangement is sometimes demanding, not only on the pocket but also on the imagination. The tendency on the part of the commercial grower is to produce millions of blooms all grown under similar conditions and all as uniform and as well-produced as possible. Added to this is the tendency in the markets for flowers to become less varied, certain limited kinds being spread over almost the entire year. Thus we can get roses, chrysanthemums, carnations and gladioli almost throughout the year and narcissi for nine months out of 12, to

Though smaller than most commercial roses the Garnette varieties are very long lasting. Complemented by foliage, they make a pretty table centre (see overleaf for stages).

1

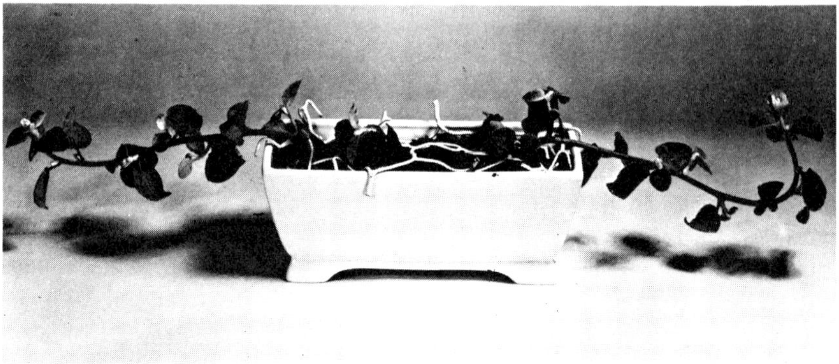

2

1 For a long low arrangement it is often best first to determine the length by arranging the longest side stems. **2** Several stems of the 'filler', *Helichrysum petiolaris* foliage are used here but ivy trails or some other small-leaved sprays can be used instead.

mention only a few examples.

This uniformity of standard is not entirely to the flower arranger's advantage. There is something very endearing about a flower which is not quite perfect by commercial standards, which has a curved stem instead of a straight one, which is a little smaller than its neighbour, which is even not quite healthy and as a result has foliage beautifully tinged with unusual colour, the effects no doubt of some virus or perhaps a mineral deficiency.

People who have to depend on bought flowers are often understandably reluctant to cut the long stems for which they have paid. But the fact is that if you do not shorten some stems you cannot arrange the flowers so that every individual is displayed. Flower arrangement is really all about getting value, value for flowers you grow, for flowers you buy. If you cannot see them all properly, and see them at their best, because they are obscuring each other, you are simply not getting value.

Cut the stems ruthlessly

So the first thing to do is to brace yourself and be prepared to cut off some of the stem from some of your flowers. As a rule stems are straight and stiff, a quality which is not easy to mask, and if you are not skilful or practised, bought flowers can look stilted and even self-conscious. Accessories will help you here, even if these are no more than a few leaves borrowed from the kitchen, such as a crinkled cabbage leaf, the coral-like sharp yellow leaves from forced rhubarb, or vivid peppers, subtle aubergines. Shells, driftwood, dried, preserved and skeletonised leaves can also be used with the flowers to help remove any stiffness. Once used, they can be stored away until they are needed again for some other occasion. Even fresh leaves can be used time and time again. Occasionally something remaining from one week's flowers can be used with the new batch, buds, leaves, flower centres or flower calyxes; for example, if dying carnation petals are pulled away a pretty little green cup remains. All these help to furnish a vase a little more fully.

Even those pieces of stem which were cut can be used. For instance I like to make a curve of narcissi on a pinholder and arrange the pieces of fluted cut stem sprayed out in a fan to left or right of the stem bases. The pieces are cut on a slant and are arranged so that the slant points away from the centre. Forced lily-of-the-valley leaves are very beautiful and these usually last long after the flowers have faded. They will go with other flowers, with any of the narcissi or with freesias, to mention only two. Group them so that they make a little skirt at the foot of the stems. The particular green harmonises very prettily with freesias, which seldom come with enough foliage on them because if the grower picked the whole stem he would also cut precious tiny buds.

Keep plenty of ivy at hand for little flowers such as these. Ivy seems to suit every flower. If you don't live near a supply of wild ivy, keep a good large house-plant going simply to provide the odd trail or two. Once the ivy has been used in an arrangement it can be struck as a cutting to make a new plant. Alternatively, keep a vase filled with moist sand and when the cut piece of ivy is not in use push it into this. Keep it in a light place and it should be in good shape for you when you want it another time.

When you go shopping for vegetables keep a watch for tiny, prettily coloured cabbages that still have good outer leaves. These can be used as a focal point in an arrangement. A few flowers can rise from behind the cabbage 'rose' at the centre in several ways, as a fan, parts of a curve or parts of a crescent. On the other hand, if you do not wish to use a whole cabbage, save the best of the leaves. These look surprisingly well with daffodils in spring and with roses, anemones and tulips.

Foliage from the florist

Florists sell a limited amount of foliage, often more in the early parts of the year than at other times. You can buy eucalyptus. Preserve some of this, giving some of the branches just a short spell in the solution—say 48 hours—so that they keep their greyish-green bloom. Keep others in longer so that they turn

almost to a purple beech colour. These will be useful later on in the autumn. Instructions for preserving foliage are given in *Long-lasting Arrangements*.

Grevillea or silk oak is another fine foliage on sale. Don't pass it over because the stems are long and you have only short or medium flowers. The individual leaves can be stripped off and used separately. These also look fine with daffodils and they suit tulips, freesias and other tiny bulb flowers. Turn some of them so that their soft, silky, grey undersides show. Grevillea is so long lasting that you can use the leaves time and time again. Even when you think they are finished you can put them between paper and press them with a hot iron. They will then be ready to store for winter arrangements. Some grevillea is dyed, but it can be treated in exactly the same way.

Golden privet on sale is much more attractive than one might realise at first glance. I have a plant in the garden and I use it frequently. Branches you buy, like the pieces you pick from the garden, need some grooming. They are usually just the wrong shape to use, but the laterals or side pieces cut away and used separately are nicely graded, leaves opposite, tapering to the tips. Use them in table arrangements for side stems or for pieces to flow over the rim below and between the flowers.

Buy blossom only if it is mainly in bud; open blossom will drop quickly. Some flowers such as narcissi and tulips are now marketed in bud. Gladioli should have only the bottom 'pip' opening. If you want them to last well put them in shallow water to restrain their energies.

Arranging gladioli

The way you arrange gladioli is important if you are to get the greatest value from them. The lower florets fade before the top buds are open, so unless the stems are carefully arranged the lower portions soon look shabby. If they are set one stem before the other, one young bloom or bud covering the lowest florets of the one behind it (though not actually resting on them) the beauty of the spikes is captured for a little longer. You can pull off the faded pips and the young bloom will fill the space for a while.

Obviously the stems in the foreground will have to be cut much shorter than the stem at the back of the arrangement. Spikes of fully-opened flowers can be cut short and used in a low arrangement, a table decoration for example. They can also be used to bring instant colour to an arrangement of newly-cut stems, the latter being arranged as suggested above, while the shortened spikes of fully opened flowers can be arranged at the base of the stems. They can be removed after a few days and replaced with leaves.

Five gladioli spikes alone will make a good decoration if you take full advantage of the leaves. These will probably have to be stripped from the stems; the grower is certain to have 'tipped' some of them, cutting off the

Even cut-off stem portions can be used decoratively, as in this autumn amaryllis arrangement. With the flowers is *Ricinus*, true castor oil plant, a good one for tubs and balconies.

little extremity of natural fading which often appears on older leaves. These cut leaves are not pretty enough to stand outlined between the spikes, but they can be bowed into one or more loops to make abstract leaf shapes. They can then be arranged at the foot of stems impaled on a pin-holder. Hold the two ends of the loop tightly between fingers and thumb and push them down between the points of the holder. Arrange them around the stems just as though they were large leaves, taking care that you bow and not bend them. Between these, contrasting them prettily, you can arrange small sword-like leaves stripped from the upper parts of the stem or perhaps tips cut from some long stem before you bow the other portion of it.

If you have no alternative but to use ready tipped leaves, re-trim them, cutting the tips on a longer slant. When you use these or uncut leaves turn them so that the slant on each leaf follows the same line, preferably inwards.

Do not be in a hurry to throw away the leaves if you are planning to make dried flower arrangements. They will sometimes take the glycerine and water solution well and will change to a pleasant silky tan. The leaves can also be pressed under the carpet between newspapers and will turn colour with this method too.

Variations on the daisy theme

Some of the cheapest flowers such as the marguerites or *Chrysanthemum maximum* go on for a long time and they are usually such a good buy that it is a pity not to make the most of them. Naturally many variations can be played on the daisy theme simply by changing their companions. These can vary from other flowers to all kinds of leaves. But sometimes try using them entirely on their own with nothing else at all, depending only on a good stylised line. You can use either pin-holders or foamed plastic for this. Try arranging them before a large sea fan, or behind a piece of coral. Try also staining their centres to match some colour theme; a touch of ink or even poster paint will do the trick.

If you like summery and informal arrangements, these single daisies look well with scarlet anemones pretending to be poppies and bleached barley bought from the florist, or wild grasses. If you store them carefully after use these can be arranged many times before they finally collapse.

Like the *Chrysanthemum maximum* pyrethrums are good long-lasting summer daisies. Don't be alarmed if when you get these home the petals seem to have turned back and the flowers appear to have wilted badly. If the centres are young—and all young daisy-like flowers in good condition should have a green or immature zone in the centre of the eye—simply stand the stems in 1–2 in. of boiling water and leave them there until it cools. You can then stand or arrange them in tepid water as recommended in *Preparation and Equipment*.

Many daisies, such as the exotic gerbera, will wilt because they have been cut while still too young. Whereas some flowers such as daffodils are best cut in bud there are others which will not respond to this treatment.

Flowers wilt, of course, when they are too old and are fading and you cannot revive these. But when you buy daisies of all kinds always check the centres.

The pyrethrums have stems which are usually more fully clothed with leaves than those of the marguerites. It is important that the stem portion which is to go under water is stripped, for these particular flowers soon turn the water sour. If you have to shorten stems of pyrethrum set the leafy cut portions aside. They are useful to arrange among the stems, thus hiding the stem-holder and also contrasting with the flowers which rise above the leaves. As a rule you can arrange this portion as you go. When the flowers have faded you can pull their petals off and use the tansy-like centres in some other arrangement.

Scabious also can be treated in much the same way. There is often no need for extra filling material. Buy bunches with long stems and plenty of leaves and buds even if you want to use them for a low arrangement such as a bowl for the table centre. As the blooms are cut from the long stems trim the leafy portions left and arrange these among the stems. Try to keep some buds on long stems so that they can make graceful lines at rim level and provide contrast between the round blooms elsewhere.

Sweet peas are enchanting but they are not really good buys because they do not last long after they have been through the rigours of both market and shop. These are flowers which could well do with being cut in bud and marketed quite young. So avoid buying them unless you see that the topmost blooms of the spray are still in bud. Arrange them in shallow water, for they last longer this way.

Chrysanthemums and dahlias

Many flowers such as godetias are bushy and these have to be streamlined for grace. Stem ends must be stripped of leaves, of course, but usually you can also strip off some of the side stems, thus providing yourself with large flowers and bud clusters on short stems.

So many spray types of stems, for instance chrysanthemums, give much greater value if they are divided carefully. One spray can be considerably pruned so that it gives a slender stem with only few flowers for the tall centre stem. Side stems taken from it can be arranged low in the decorations or used elsewhere in a completely different style of arrangement.

So far as dahlias are concerned, it is quite often the opposite. You can often buy wonderful blooms in lovely colours but with very short stems. You can make tall arrangements from these by using 'towered' blocks of OASIS, one piece on another. Dahlias go into this stem-holding medium very well. You can also use small tablet or cigar tubes wide enough to take three stems. These can be spliced to a short cane which is then arranged like any other stem. The flowers are arranged in the tube, which should be half-filled with the crumbled wet plastic. It is possible to lash a block of plastic to two canes, one on each side of it, for the same purpose. You can hide any means you have employed to lift the flowers by arranging others in front of the mechanics.

Freesias are seldom marketed with their own foliage; here a trail of variegated ivy cut from a house-plant has been introduced, with a leaf from *Begonia rex* and one from the wild herb Robert. Opposite: Silk oak is often on sale; it is both graceful and long lasting. A framework of leaves and driftwood such as this can be used for weeks on end, while the flowers are changed as they fade.

Long, low baskets like trugs suit dahlias and they also look well arranged with fruits. But be wary of arranging apples with flowers in general—the gas given off by the ripe fruit has an inhibiting effect on some kinds. Carnations, for example, will go 'sleepy' if there are ripe apples nearby. Grapes, tomatoes, peppers, aubergines and berries of all kinds including branches of blackberries will all suit dahlias and can safely be used.

Orchids are an investment

Chincherinchees are a good buy, even though they may have to be imported from South Africa; some are now produced in Britain. They are very long lasting and it sometimes takes five or six weeks for the flower spike to open fully. Keep the lower florets snipped off as they fade or the arrangement may begin to look shabby. In winter these flowers look particularly attractive when used with the dark green and black clusters of ivy berries. These ivy

fruits last well and often those you gather for one arrangement will do for more to come. Keep an eye open for these and for other berries when you go into the country.

Orchids are nothing like as expensive as they seem, simply because they last so long. A spray of cymbidiums or two or three slipper orchids, cypripediums, look lovely in *pot-et-fleur* arrangements; so in fact do all smooth-stemmed flowers.

POT-ET-FLEUR

The recently acquired knowledge that plants do not have to be grown in a terracotta pot with a hole in its base has led to a change in our entire concept of how plants can be displayed. And thanks to progress in greenhouse production there is now a great range of inexpensive pot plants from which to choose. Some you can grow yourself from seed or cuttings.

My own interest in mixing cut flowers and pot plants came from a natural tendency to embellish and generally tidy-up! Someone had given me a bowl of mixed plants for Christmas and by early spring it was looking tired so I 'arranged' it, bringing in a fresh plant and inducing it to 'bloom' by incorporating cut flowers with the existing foliage. The improvement was instant and even dramatic.

It occurred to me that rather than beginning with a fading bowl it would be worth while building an arrangement which was a blend of both flower arrangement and plant decor. This seemed to be a natural projection of the art of flower arrangement. *Pot-et-fleur*, as such arrangements have come to be called, is something which appeals particularly to the man and woman who lik to grow plants rather than merely to cut them.

Pot-et-fleur arrangements are highly individual and they never are anythink like so hackneyed as many styles of flower arrangement have become. One accepts the plants as they are. There is seldom any pruning, shaping or denuding. As you would expect, you often need to tilt, angle or coax to get them to assume the position you require, but nearly always the arranger has to fit in with the plant rather than the other way round. The main concern should be that the plants are arranged in such a way that besides looking lovely and contributing to the decoration as a whole, they will continue to grow happily for a reasonably long period.

This is where the arranger who has a greenhouse or conservatory, or even a suitable window-sill, has an advantage, for tired plants can be removed and given a period of rejuvenation before they are used again.

Containers can be as varied as they are for flower arrangements except that generally they need to be deep enough to hide the rim of the flower pots. However, it is possible sometimes to hide these behind driftwood, cork, bark, stones or pebbles.

Planning for later additions

Generally speaking I prefer to arrange individual pots rather than to plant them, but this depends on circumstances. Pots may be tilted (an essential for cryptanthus and other rosette plants which look so well as a focal point) by wedging pebbles under them or by using a piece of OASIS as a holder and securing them in this by pushing them in at the required angle. The plastic is kept moist and in this way helps to succour the plant without swamping it. Secondhand crumbly plastic left over from flower arrangements is also good for packing plants in place, as are also peat and sand.

If you prefer to plant a bowl with plants knocked from their pots then be sure also to plant one or more empty flower pots as well as a container or two for cut flowers. If you do this at the time of planting you will not damage the roots of the existing plants when you come to change the bowl's contents, or if you wish to add another plant or perhaps a short-stemmed posy of flowers to add a knot of colour.

Naturally one must use what plants are available, but if you are starting from scratch keep the few basic rules of flower arrangement in mind. Colours need to harmonise and you will find that there are many more hues in a green plant than you might realise. Look, for example, at leaf-stem, bracts or stipules and also on the undersides of the foliage. You may find magenta, ruby, violet or even blue, and from these hues, no matter how small the amount, you can take your cue when choosing flowers to go with the plants and decide which of these hues to accent.

The most suitable flowers

The more colourful the foliage of the plants the more simple your flowers can be. Those which grow from bulbs and corms, such as narcissi, lilies, gladioli and freesias, are the most suitable. Arums are 'naturals' since so many house-plants are aroids. Orchids always look well; their stems are uncluttered and their shapes sculpted. Greenhouse carnations, orchids and garden peonies and dahlias look delightfully opulent and their colours blend well with the plants. Roses look rich but are sometimes too leafy and so tend to confuse the outline. Tulips need to lose some of their leaves. (A *pot-et-fleur* arrangement incorporating tulips, incidentally, is shown on the cover.)

The flowers themselves can be arranged in a variety of means according to what space there may be in the main vessel for their containers. In some cases it is best to arrange each stem in a separate container, a cigar or tablet tube perhaps, either of which can easily be pushed down into the soil or foamed plastic. The conical metal vases sold by florists' sundriesmen are useful because being green they can be easily disguised or hidden and because they can be so well anchored. It is sometimes advisable, however, to fill them with a stem-holder.

Small pieces of driftwood are invaluable, not only for hiding the rim of a flower pot (the curve of the wood can follow the curve of the pot) but also for linking one component with another. Small pieces, arranged to look like one unit, come in useful here. Driftwood can also support climbing plants in an attractive way. You can fix, say, a *Philodendron scandens* to a tall piece of driftwood and arrange flowers in tubes hidden behind the wood. It is preferable to other woods because it is sterile and not likely to contain pests

Left: Orchids are a good buy and are extremely long lasting. Arranged with them here are winter-flowering plum and ornamental kale. Below: In this *pot-et-fleur* arrangement, the gladioli can be replaced when they have faded. Both the philodendron and the begonia can be used as they are many times before being given a rest.

of any kind.

Hidden aids: Plants knocked from their pots should be planted in a good compost so that they thrive and those which are plunged in their pots should be fed from time to time. One essential item is charcoal. Fortunately this is easy and cheap to buy at hardware stores, chemists' and garden centres; it can be used again and again. This forms a good drainage medium if you place a generous layer on the floor of your container, it has the additional advantage that it absorbs any noxious odours that might arise from the small amounts of stale water that might possibly collect at the base of the container.

If you use a plant which should be kept on the dry side, such as a cactus or sansevieria, first envelope its pot in a polythene bag so that excess moisture is kept from the roots. The bag can easily be hidden.

Once the arrangement is completed spray the contents from time to time with clean water, especially if some of the plant pots are tilted and hence difficult to water properly. Most flowers will also enjoy this. And don't forget, the moment a plant looks tired, to take it out and replace it with a new one. This way your *pot-et-fleur* will never be a 'still life' but always full of interest and colour.

9 HAPPY HOUSE-PLANTS

Two common misconceptions about house-plants are that in the first place they require a great deal of attention and secondly, that as a result of this they will live almost for ever. Neither of these suppositions is true.

When we plant a shrub in the garden (most house-plants are shrubs) we take the normal protective steps to make sure that it gets off to a good start, but after this it is more or less on its own. We check it occasionally to make sure that it does not need water, that it is not infested with pests or that it is not broken or misshapen, but on the whole it has to learn to make its own way in life. If it fails, if it turns out to be sickly, unproductive of blossom or fruit, unhappy in appearance or demanding of too much time or labour, then out it comes and it is replaced by another plant. Because there are so many plants in the garden we cannot afford to be over-sentimental about just one of them.

But indoors we are closer to our plants in our day-to-day lives; we get to know them, one by one, almost like pets and they steal their way into our hearts so that unless we control ourselves we tend to treat them that way too. We fuss over them, over-feed them, over-water them, move them around and given them no opportunity to settle down and get used to their surroundings.

It is true that house-plants, living as they do under highly artificial conditions, require more attention and care than the trees and shrubs outside in their natural surroundings, but no real house-plant should demand more than two or three minutes' attention a week. I manage to live with and enjoy rather more than 100 plants in my home in the country and I give them an average of only about half an hour a week. This is partly because of many years of experience, partly because the house is particularly suited to their care and partly because I am (just) able to steal myself into throwing out plants which have become sickly or unproductive of bloom through old age, and beginning again with new—in short, to regard house-plants as a means of decoration which must be treated as expendable. But on the other hand this is not to say that some of the plants here are not more than ten years old and have in their time demanded considerable time and attention to see them through a particularly bad patch.

What is a 'house-plant'?

Almost any plants can be dug up from the soil, placed in a pot and brought indoors. Here most plants will last for a few days, some for longer. But on the whole by house-plants we mean those that will live for long periods, probably months, under normal home conditions of light, warmth and humidity.

Most house-plants then, under this meaning of the term, will be foliage plants, grown for the beauty of their leaves, the colour, texture, shape or habit. A few will be grown both for their flowers and their foliage and examples here that come quickly to mind are the grave and glorious Greek vase plant, *Aechmea rhodocyanea*, with its long-lasting and prickly pink flower stem and blue flowers, the zebra plant or aphelandra with its cockscomb of yellow flower and its striped leaves, the striking 'crown of thorns', surprisingly a euphorbia, with its tiny, red blood-spots of flowers and the tender and lovely African violet, furry-leaved and never without a top knot or froth of nonchalant flowers the whole year through.

Yet we must make exceptions for such flowering plants as azaleas and begonias, for the ever-widening range of bulbous plants which can be grown indoors to give us magnificent blooms, and even for the little early primrose or snowdrop, dug up from the garden to be brought inside as a promise that spring is near.

If we accept that flowering plants of this and other kinds are to be enjoyed in the home while they look their best, and are then to be thrown out or to be re-planted in the garden, then surely we can accept that all other plants in the home can stay only when they are decorative, and that when they have passed their best or outgrown their situation they should be discarded. An elderly or ailing plant has ceased to be decorative and it is most unlikely that it will ever again be beautiful. But even worse is the fact that such a plant will be particularly sensitive to pest or disease attack and so possibly a source of infection for many of the other plants which may be around it.

Light is the first necessity

When you buy your replacement plant, make a change from the very wide range of house-plants available today. Do not buy a plant that is too delicate and exotic unless you have 'green fingers' or are prepared for it to last only a short time. But there are many house-plants out of the ordinary run which are easy to grow and will live happily with you for many months.

Some people see a house-plant which strikes their imagination and they buy it, take it home and then wander about trying to find a place for it, one that suits it both physically and aesthetically. Others have a place already vacant in their homes and they set out to buy a plant to fit this place. Which is correct? Both.

But a little guidance may be helpful. The most vital necessity for house-plants is neither warmth nor water but light. The plants which need the greatest amount and intensity of light are cacti, some of the few plants that will revel in direct and baking sunshine. All flowering plants and all plants with variegated foliage require good light. Sun coming through a south-facing window will be too strong for them, but not if it comes from the east or west. Plants needing the least light are those with thick or fleshy dark green leaves.

Moderate, moist conditions

With very few exceptions high temperatures are neither necessary nor liked by most plants. Certainly no plant should ever be placed near a fire or a radiator of any kind merely to ensure that it is kept warm. As a rule temperatures which are comfortable for humans are also comfortable for

Cacti and some succulents need a great amount and intensity of light. In the right place they will live for years. Some, like this *Sedum morganianum*, grow to a fine size.

house-plants, so one should aim for a fairly steady 65–70°F or 18–21°C.

Where rooms tend to get overheated and perhaps smoky during the evening it is best that plants are removed during the day and placed where they will have cooler and less polluted conditions. Some plants, cyclamen for example, will always do better in a lower temperature than a high one. To retain these plants in good condition for long periods, it is advisable to keep them in bedrooms or in other parts of the house where higher temperatures are not reached at certain times of the day.

Central heating is good for plants in that it gives them a comparatively steady warmth day and night and at all times of the year, but it is bad in that it dries the air and destroys the natural humidity that the plants need. This humidity, incidentally, is also good for furniture and indeed for the human skin, so in every way it is worth while trying to increase it. Fortunately this is a comparatively simple matter. A few pans of water about the house will add appreciably to the humidity and they can be hidden or disguised easily enough. Radiator troughs are available very cheaply and these perform their task perfectly adequately without resorting to the sometimes very expensive electric humidifiers on the market.

Ways of providing humidity: But it is even simpler and in some ways more efficient to give localised humidity to each and every plant that really needs it. This is done by plunging the plant, a term which means sinking the plant pot inside another, larger, waterproof container which holds peat, sand, crumbled FLORAPAK or any similar material that will absorb quantities of water. By doing this two results are achieved. In the first place any excess water from the flower pot will drain off into the packing material and secondly, when this is damp it will give off moisture by evaporation and this will rise to envelope the plant foliage in a tiny micro-climate of warm, moist air, just the treatment it likes and needs.

So beneficial are the results of plunging plant pots inside these peat-filled outer containers that as a general rule it is wise and helpful for all house-plants to be so treated. There is the added advantage that the outer pots can be considerably more decorative than the normal plant pots, plastic or terracotta, and fitting into the general decor and colouring of the room.

A further means of providing the necessary humidity for certain plants is actually to spray them with clean tepid water, using a fine spray or atomiser that will project the water more as a mist than as actual droplets. A spray of this type can damage certain furnishings, so it should be used only where there is no fear of this happening or where it is possible to protect the background by means of a few sheets of newspaper or some similar shielding material. The spraying need be only very light, certainly not sufficient to cause drips, but this light misting will be enormously beneficial to the plants.

Yet another method of increasing general humidity is by producing steam. In some rooms it will be possible, once a week or so, to boil a kettle for a few minutes or to bring into the room a large saucepan of boiling water and leave it to cool. There will be a significant increase in the humidity and all plants in the room will benefit.

A more local steam treatment can be given to certain plants such as saintpaulias or African violets perhaps once a month, if it is suspected that the atmophere is too dry for them. Place the plant inside a slightly larger but waterproof bowl, if it is not already in a plunge pot. Stand this in the centre of a large basin and then pour in boiling water so that the steam rises around and envelops the plant yet the boiling water itself cannot damage the roots. Leave the plant there until the water cools.

Don't over-water

The question of watering is a difficult one to answer. Most newcomers to the art of indoor gardening would like to be told that this plant will require watering once a week, and that one twice, but such directions are impossible to give. They depend on weather, the warmth of the house, the amount and intensity of light, the quantity and quality of the water, the size and type of the plant and other matters. Watering is really a matter of knowing the plant and this comes only with experience. But it is worth knowing that more plants die of over-watering than any other mistreatment. For this reason it is wise to err on the side of meanness rather than generosity. It is always possible to give a little more water if the plant is seen to be dry, but much more difficult to remove water from a drowning plant.

The most efficient way to water a plant is to submerge the entire pot in a bath or pail of water and leave it there until the bubbles have ceased to rise from the soil surface, an indication that all the air spaces in the soil have been filled with water. If the pot is then removed from the water and stood on one side to drain, water will flow away from the drainage holes at the base of the pot; when water rushes out from one end it sucks air after it through the soil at the top of the pot.

Plants must have air as well as water at the roots. Giving little driblets of water to the pot from time to time does not encourage this surge of fresh air through the soil, so if the plant cannot be moved to submerge the pot entirely, it is wise to water sufficiently to allow water to trickle through the drainage holes. Leave this excess water in the saucer or other container for a couple of hours or so, in case the soil absorbs it again. But if it still remains after this time it should be thrown away, otherwise it will help the plant roots to drown. If the plant pot is plunged inside another container containing some moisture-retentive material, then any excess water will be absorbed by this and released gently and slowly through the pot to the roots again and to the air in the form of evaporation.

The water requirements of house-plants vary according to the season. Most plants are more or less dormant during the darker days of winter. It is then that they take their rest and at this time they require only sufficient water to keep the soil just moist, no more. If more water is given the roots cannot absorb it and tend to show their rejection by becoming mildewed, even rotten.

There are plants, however, which continue to grow through winter, for example saintpaulias. These plants obviously need more water than if they were dormant but not so much as they would require in summer. There are even one or two plants, such as the vigorous and fast-growing vine tetrastigma, which has reversed seasons and rests during summer, while it grows rampantly during winter. Obviously here too watering should follow the plant's requirements.

When to feed and prune

Feeding follows exactly the same pattern. A plant needs feeding most when it is growing most and this period is probably in late spring or early summer. During the winter rest period no food at all should be given to house-plants.

Just as it is a good rule to give too little rather than too much water, so it is wise to give too little rather than too much food. This is for two reasons. In the first place over-feeding a plant is just as unwise as over-feeding a human. It leads to digestive troubles. But where a human can protest or can leave a part of the food set before him, a plant cannot. Secondly, over-feeding leads to over-growth and this is a strain on the plant and a nuisance to the indoor gardener, who finds suddenly that a certain plant has outgrown its situation and is an embarrassment rather than a pleasure. Success with house-plants does not mean growing them to huge size but keeping them small and slow-growing while they retain their looks and their health.

A number of house-plants, particularly the climbers and trailers,

Left: 'Plunging' a pot inside another more decorative one which has been lined with peat will help to create humidity. Above: This handsome *Philodendron pinnatifidum* is several years old and has lived in the same pot for most of its life.

frequently benefit from a certain amount of pruning and training. This keeps them under control and suitable for their surroundings. Tradescantias, for example, become brown and straggly if their trails are allowed to grow too long. They should be nipped off while still at their best; the excess portion can always be rooted again, in the same pot if necessary. Ivies, cissus and rhoicissus, and some of the philodendrons will all react well to a certain degree of pruning.

Some good-tempered house-plants

All of the most popular and most frequently seen house-plants are remarkably tolerant and easy to handle. As a general rule it is only when one turns to some of the more exotic and glamorous plants that one runs into trouble, usually because humidity and high temperatures are lacking.

For the very beginner or for the person who is so demoralised by a series of failures with house-plants as to be fearful of making any further attempt, any of the following plants can be recommended (for a description, see the alphabetical list at the end of this book).

Aechmea rhodocyanea	*Chlorophytum comosum*	*Cissus antarctica*
Fatshedera lizei	*Ficus schryveriana*	Hederas or ivies (any)
Philodendron scandens	*Rhoicissus rhomboidea*	*Sanseviera trifasciata laurentii*
Araucaria excelsa	*Aspidistra lurida*	

This sounds like a much more formidable group than it really is; all these plants are really easy to handle, all will live for months, if not years, and from them it is possible to select a plant for almost any situation or location in the home.

It will be noted that only one flowering plant is included. This is because there are very few flowering house-plants which are decorative for long periods yet are comparatively foolproof for the beginner. The only exception in the list is the aechmea which will produce a flower which is actually a single stem or scape bearing many flowers. The flowers themselves have a comparatively brief life but the prickly and highly decorative scape will live on for weeks if not months. Bulb flowers such as tulips and hyacinths and those such as cyclamen which are grown from corms are dealt with in *Bulbs through the Year*.

Unless we purposely specify to the contrary and are prepared to pay extra, all house-plants are marketed small and immature. This way we have the pleasure of watching them grow and at the same time they are able to adjust themselves to the changes in atmosphere and surroundings in their new homes.

The aechmea, araucaria, aspidistra, and also the chlorophytum and sansevieria will never grow to unmanageable proportions, although over the years some may double or more in size. The ficus, a more decorative form of the rubber plant, will grow to a tree that will reach the ceiling. The remaining plants are climbers or trailers and depending on how they are grown and trained will cover a wall, decorate an archway, fill in a division or make a screen. Some will need support but the ivies will, if you wish, attach themselves to your indoor walls and work their decorative way up to and across the ceiling. They do little harm to the basic fabric of the house but they do make things difficult when decorating. If removed they will take paint and paper with them, so unless you are an avid plant-lover or relaxed, informal and tolerant in your ideas of home decoration, you may be wise to control your plant and restrain it from climbing. Otherwise, particularly if you live in a city, you may have to choose between putting off redecorating a grimy ceiling or tearing down your cherished plant.

Humans come before plants

It is helpful also to remember that a plant will always turn its face to the light. This means that where a plant grows directly in a window it will tend to turn its back to the room and its inhabitants. This can be avoided with some plants by turning them each day so that they get equal light on all sides, but where the plant is too large for this, or has begun to climb, this will be impossible. So with this habit in mind it is well if possible to grow a climber on the wall facing a window, so that the foliage always faces into the room.

As a rule it will be found practical only to place comparatively small plants right in the window spaces. Too large plants get in the way and they also restrict the amount of light entering the room. Small plants next to the glass need to be turned so that they get equal amounts of light on each side and so grow straight. The best way is to give each plant pot a quarter turn each day.

Do try to bear in mind the fact that humans come before plants. If any plant interferes with the comfort or convenience of any person in the home then it is in the wrong place. If any plant occupies a permanent position for so long that it builds up behind it a little residue of dead leaves, dust and even dead flies, then once again it is in the wrong position, for this is an invitation to disease. On the other hand, don't tuck away a plant so that it is difficult to see and enjoy properly or so that it is difficult to tend and water, for this will mean that it will be neglected.

Once you get to know your plants you will be able to decide yourself which plant will be suitable for growing in the living room, which for kitchen, bedroom or perhaps bathroom. You will have to decide on the basis of such decorative factors as suitability, colour and texture, space and on such horticultural factors as light intensity, warmth, relative humidity, space and ease of handling.

Cold and dark halls

In many homes the hall is inclined to be rather dark, cool in winter and possibly subjected to icy draughts when the door is opened for more than a few moments. These limitations determine that only a comparatively tough plant can live and flourish and that one must select with care and knowledge any plant destined to spend more than a week or two at a time in such a situation. Fortunately, certain plants will accept poor conditions for a limited period so long as a longer spell of good conditions follows; in other words we can set them down in a cold and dark place and enjoy them there for a brief period, so long as we remove them to a place with better light and greater warmth for a period of recuperation. Other plants will so resent this chop and change behaviour that they will give up the ghost at a very early stage.

Of the group of easy plants listed earlier, araucaria, aspidistra, ficus and some of the hederas would probably exist in the cold and dark, all of them doing better if they could have an occasional holiday in the light and warmth.

From the humanitarian point of view, however, why should a plant, any plant, be placed in a situation where it will be subjected to almost intolerable conditions and where it will hardly be seen? Much better surely to place a

Plants always face the light. Those which grow in or near a window should be turned frequently so that they grow evenly. This trough holds cyclamen, chrysanthemums and vinca.

Many types of plants will grow happily in a warm sitting room. Stand those which need most light, usually the flowering kinds like these primulas, nearest the glass.

dried flower decoration, an engaging lamp or an eye-catching picture in such a position.

Living rooms and kitchens

The most popular room of the house, the living room, demands almost as careful a choice of plants because it will almost certainly fluctuate in temperature, becoming increasingly warm at the end of the day until everyone has gone to bed and cooling off suddenly almost to hall temperature. At the same time it may be subjected to clouds of tobacco smoke and probably fluctuations of humidity, depending on the presence or absence of a number of perspiring human figures. Given that the room has good light, any and all of the plants mentioned in the 'easy group' list will be successful in such a room. Indeed, they have been chosen primarily with such a room in mind.

In the kitchen we come suddenly face to face with a problem that may possibly affect the entire house. If cooking or water heating is by gas, indeed if room warming is by gas fire rather than by a more remote gas central heating, it is certain that a minute amount of gas will be entering the atmosphere and doing a great deal of harm to all but the toughest of your house-plants. Most plants are intensely sensitive to atmospheric pollution and even the tiniest amount of domestic gas in the atmosphere will affect many of them.

An efficiently ventilated kitchen, however, will permit plants to be grown in the vicinity of a gas appliance and many plants, including even some culinary herbs, can grow for long periods quite happily here. Much will depend on the availability of light, heat and humidity. The latter is sometimes a regular part of the environment of some kitchens, which can enable the happy and comfortable growth of certain plants which might otherwise need special care. But space in the kitchen is usually at a premium and the kind of clinical cleanliness demanded by some housewives may lead to the banishing of house-plants, with their earthy flavour, from the sterile scene.

Bedrooms and bathrooms

Bedrooms are a different matter. In most homes, barring only the most Spartan where the windows are open all day and the curtains flap in the hygienic and virtuous wind, this is the best room in the house for house-plants. There is usually good light and some slight degree of warmth which varies very little at different times of the day. The humidity is comparatively high, compared with the warmer and more heavily inhabited parts of the house, and there is usually space for a plant to spread itself without being in the way. Unfortunately, except in the case of the bedridden—a very different circumstance—plants in a bedroom can only be admired and enjoyed for a matter of a few minutes out of every 24 hours.

In recent years there has been a rather charming fashion for growing house-plants in the bathroom. This has, I imagine, come as a result of the incidence of large bathrooms converted from the bedrooms of Victorian homes. Some of the modern plumbed cupboards called bathrooms are hardly large enough to get into ourselves, let alone share with a plant or two. But whatever the reason, the fashion is both acceptable botanically and admirable aesthetically, for most bathrooms are either white or in light tints that produce excellent light intensity. They also produce and harbour great quantities of steam, thus producing a humid atmosphere which is the delight of almost all house-plants.

Here, in the bathroom (so long as there is space and so long as the water is not heated by a localised gas system) is the place for one or two tender African violets, for a sensitive little pilea or a gorgeous chocolate and green maranta.

Choosing the right spot

Choose as carefully as you can the position in your home for your plants. Look first for the quality of the light available, for it is not difficult to make a room warmer or cooler, or more humid, but you cannot increase the intensity of the light which falls on a plant. For years I had a pretty little variegated ivy growing in an antique water pitcher in a corner of my bedroom. It was healthy and attractive but it refused to grow. I tried more water and less, more food and less, but to no effect. Then I moved it across the room and placed it right in a south-facing window and in a matter of a few months it had grown some 4 ft.

As well as demanding plenty of light, practically all house-plants also need freedom from draughts. Cold draughts or hot draughts, it makes no difference, both are highly damaging. So if your plant is in a window make quite sure that the frame is well fitting. Equally, if it is somewhere near a fire, radiator or other heating appliance, make quite sure that the rising hot air does not sweep around your plant.

On the whole, however, once a plant has been given a position in the home into which it can settle comfortably it should give you little or no trouble. This is not to say that plants can be left alone for long periods. Obviously they require feeding and watering and the best thing to do is to establish a regular routine for these activities. If you make a habit of going around your plants at the same time on the same day once or twice a week you will find that you cut down the time you need to give them and you enormously increase your prospects for success. The little occasional dribble of water into this pot or that, the odd drop or two of plant food on the spur of the moment, these things can so quickly add up to a plant dying of drowning or of burnt roots. But if these attentions are given regularly, then it is a simple matter to remember.

Checking and cleaning

When each plant is watered and fed at its appointed time, just check over the flowers or the foliage to make quite sure all is well. Look for distorted or discoloured leaves, for portions of the plant that appear to droop, look for falling leaves and inspect the plant quickly to make sure that no insect pests are visible, looking particularly at the tender growing shoots. An examination of this sort need take only a few seconds, but it can discover, identify, check and correct many possible troubles that might occur far more seriously in the future.

But although you go over all your plants at one time this does not mean that all must be treated alike. You may find that one plant is actually flagging for want of water while another has a soil surface moist both in appearance and to the touch and so needs no water at all. One plant may have shed a leaf or two in the normal process of growing while another may have shed a leaf or two as an indication that it is sickening. A little observation and experience will soon tell you which is which.

Some plants tend to collect dust on their leaves, depending on the size of the leaves and the amount of dust in the atmosphere. Obviously a home in a busy city or an industrial centre is likely to have more dust than one out

in the cleaner air of the countryside. This dust can clog the breathing pores, the stomata, in the leaves and cause the plant to sicken. So both for the health of the plant and its appearance it is well to give most plants an occasional clean.

These *Cryptanthus zonatus,* or earth stars, are best watered by spraying the foliage with an atomiser. There should always be water in the little central 'well' at the plant's heart.

Where there are large leaves—such as those of an india rubber plant or a Swiss cheese plant—this is a comparatively simple matter, for the leaves are few in number and quite easily swabbed down. Use a tissue or a soft sponge and tepid rain water. Never use olive oil, milk or anything else that is likely to clog the pores even more or which will collect even more dust. If you like the leaves to shine, you can use one of the several AEROSOL sprays on the market after having cleaned them with rain water. Do bear in mind that some dust, particularly that deposited in cities and industrial areas, can be sharp and gritty. If rubbed off the leaves too vigorously this abrasive dust can do real harm. Instead try to clean the leaves gently, using plenty of water. I suggest rain water mainly because it is soft and it does not leave any of the lime or chlorine deposits sometimes seen after using tap water.

When you go away

It is easy enough, then, to care for our plants when we are able to give them regular attention, but what is to happen to them when we leave home for a holiday or for some other reason? This can be a real problem, particularly because holidays usually take place at a time of year when warm weather and bright sunshine make greater than usual demands on the watering can.

The best answer is to have a friend, relative or neighbour to come in and look after your plants for you, having made quite sure that he or she understands what is required. (We all know of the damage that well-meaning friends can do on such occasions.) If this suggestion is impractical, then consider sending the plants to a local nursery, much as you might send the dog to a boarding kennels. Many nurseries either operate a scheme along these lines or will agree to take in 'boarders' for brief periods.

But sometimes this again is impossible. Indeed some of your plants may be too large or too firmly fixed in position to allow them to be moved. Then you have to improvise some means of seeing that your plants are watered (don't worry about feeding) until you can get back to them. The important matter here is the length of your absence. One week need cause no worry at all, two weeks is a comparatively easy time to manage, but after this things begin to get more difficult.

The first thing is to move all plants out of south or west windows and if light is vital to them place them instead in a north or east window, preferably the first. Lack of good light will not hurt most plants for a couple of weeks or so and will considerably reduce the quantity of moisture that they will require.

Solving the watering problem: Small plants can be watered well and then enveloped completely, pot, foliage and all, inside a transparent plastic bag which should then be sealed. And along the same lines, if a plant is too large for treatment of this kind, it may be possible to envelope the pot only so as to reduce the amount of evaporation from the pot. By using a very large plastic bag it is possible to make a temporary indoor greenhouse to hold several plants; it can be propped into a tent-like shape with two or three broom handles or garden canes.

It is possible also to take certain moveable plants and place them in the bath or in a sink. If this contains just an inch or two of water it is probable that the damage done by the brief period of semi-drowning will be outweighed by the benefit of being kept moist until the water has evaporated sufficiently to allow the roots to breathe again.

There are now drip-watering appliances on the market which really are effective and almost foolproof. These usually consist of a reservoir (sometimes called a 'glug bottle' for obvious reasons) placed high and a number of feeder tubes leading from it to the soil surfaces of the various pots. These tubes have a number of adjustable nozzles so that you can decide the amount of water to be released into each pot.

An alternative method which is both more expensive and more effective follows the same principle, the plant pots resting on a sand or pebble base which is kept constantly moist by the trickle tubes. This necessitates a comparatively large tray or bowl to hold the sand.

A holiday in the garden: There is, however, still another means available to us for keeping our house-plants moist and in good health during a temporary absence from home. This method costs nothing and is highly effective. Here one merely collects all the plants which can safely be moved and takes them out to the garden. In a shaded position they are plunged in soil or in a special bed of moist peat and the soil surface is liberally sprinkled with slug pellets. In summer weather these plants will almost without exception benefit from their spell out of doors.

Most house-plants enjoy nothing more than to be put out in a gentle summer shower. Some plants can be left outside during the whole of the summer, but in this case to take special care that they are not attacked by insects, slugs or snails. There will usually be an appreciable improvement in their appearance when you take them indoors again towards the end of the summer and certainly before any frosts may be expected. Some plants may even have grown to the extent that their roots are growing out of the pot or that they no longer fit comfortably into the space vacated when they moved out to the garden.

In the latter case it is sometimes possible to prune certain plants, particularly climbers, to keep them neat and shapely. If re-potting is required make sure always that the roots go into a new pot only one size larger than the old one. This is important, for house-plants need to be slightly pot-bound, to have their roots curled and cosy in the pot that is their home.

How and when to re-pot

No house-plant suffers from having its roots examined. Take the pot and turn it upside down with the fingers over the soil and the plant projecting between the first and second fingers. Then give the edge of the pot a sharp tap on some firm surface. The root ball will fall out of the pot into the hand. (Make sure, incidentally, that the soil is comparatively moist when doing this or dry soil from the surface will tend to be shaken out.) If the plant needs re-potting you will see that the roots are curled tightly around the perimeter of the ball and that almost all of the soil appears to have disappeared. And if on the other hand there still appears plenty of space and plenty of soil for the roots, then you can slip the root ball back into the pot and it will have come to no harm.

When re-potting, make sure first that the drainage hole or holes at the base are not so large that the compost will fall through. Today most pots are of plastic and have a series of smaller holes rather than one large one in the centre. Then scatter in ½ in. or so of good compost. This can be John Innes Potting Compost, available in small quantities from many chain stores and nearly all garden centres or it can be one of the peat-based soil-less composts such as KERIMURE or LEVINGTON. Do not mix the two types, or try to re-pot a plant in a different type of mixture.

Slip the root ball into the pot on top of the ½ in. of soil on the base of the new pot and then sprinkle more soil around the root ball and inside the pot to fill the space between the two. Firm the soil well with the thumbs and fingers and add more soil until the surface is about ½ in. from the rim of the pot. This will give space for watering. Water the re-potted plant well and then stand it in a cool, shaded place for a few days to recover.

Changing the soil: This is all very well, you may say, but what am I going to do about my rubber plant that nearly reaches the ceiling, and what about the cissus that is trained to cover the wall? Obviously these plant pots cannot be picked up and handled in the same way as just described, so we have to find some other means of refreshing or renewing the soil in these pots without even moving them from their static positions.

These large pots and even many small ones can gain a considerable 'shot in the arm' by changing just some of the soil. Gently scrape away some of the soil on the surface, ½ in., 1 in. or even more if the roots are not yet obstructing you. Scrape away this soil and throw it in the garden, certainly do not attempt to use it again for any pot plant. Then add fresh John Innes compost or other appropriate planting medium to the top of the pot to replace that you have removed. Firm it down and do not let the level become so high that watering is a problem. Once again water thoroughly and then leave the plant alone until the soil is almost bone dry before you water again.

Given careful watering and feeding many plants will live for years in the same pot. It may be true that they will grow more vigorously and more quickly if they are re-potted more frequently, but this is not always an advantage. So long as the plants remain in good health and attractive appearance they are continuing to serve you well.

Is it thirsty or drowning?

Few house-plants suffer from ill health except as a result of mistreatment. More plants die from the over-generosity of the owner than any other

Cacti and some succulents grow well together. Both these kinds of plants sometimes become infested with mealy bug, so inspect the plants regularly.

cause, usually from overwatering. A plant which is drowning reveals its discomfort first by listless behaviour, a failure to grow or to shine. Then one or two of the lower leaves begin to turn colour and after a while will drop. If the roots are examined they may even be turning mouldy.

Unfortunately many of the symptoms of a plant which is suffering acute thirst are the same as those for a plant which is drowning, the same yellowing leaves and the same fall. So you will have to search your conscience to see whether you have in fact been giving your plant too much or too little water. In the latter case it can happen that a brief and accidental period of neglect is followed by more reasonable care. But during this period of neglect the root ball has dried out to the extent that subsequent watering cannot be absorbed by the brick-hard soil or peat mixture. So although you appear to be watering correctly, in fact the plant is not able to absorb the water. It needs a good soaking in a bucket of water to get the soil into a state again where it can absorb moisture.

But although there is a fairly quick and easy way to cure a plant which is too dry at the roots, there can be no quick and easy correction of a state of drowning. Obviously watering will have to cease for a period, but apart from this little can be done except the kill-or-cure method of knocking the plant from its pot and re-potting in dry soil, after scraping away as much as possible of the old over-wet compost. This may succeed and it may not, depending mainly on the strength of the plant.

DISEASES AND PESTS

What fungal or virus diseases attack house-plants come mainly as a result of bad treatment. They are not easy to diagnose or to cure and in general it is advisable to throw the plant out and begin again. Even if you were able to save the plant it is doubtful if it would ever be the same again and there would always be great danger that it might pass on some of its weaknesses to neighbouring plants.

Pests, as opposed to diseases, are quite few in number and comparatively easy to clear. The easiest both to recognise and to deal with is the ubiquitous aphid, usually greenfly but occasionally blackfly.

Greenfly are not always easy to see unless you examine your plants very thoroughly and very frequently. The first evidence is likely to be a curious twisting or warping of certain tender shoots and possibly a change in colour. Immediate action is called for directly the pests are found, for they can multiply at an astonishing rate and could do great damage to all your indoor plants if not attacked at once.

If the attack is a light one, that is to say if only one plant is affected it may be possible to deal with it in position. A light spray with an AEROSOL fly killer will kill the greenfly also. But keep a careful watch on all the house-plants in the vicinity to make sure that other greenfly do not appear in the next few days.

A word of warning about pesticides. All garden pesticides are what they say: garden pesticides. They must never be used in the house. They are poisons and although safe to be used out of doors you will nevertheless be advised on the label to avoid getting any of the liquid or the spray on the skin and always to wash carefully after using them. So, never ever use a garden insecticide in the house in the form of a spray. The only way any can be safely used is when a systemic insecticide is watered in weak solution on to the soil of certain plants. Systemics are absorbed by the roots and carried in the sap to all parts of the plant. Aphids are suckers, so when they suck at the sap they become poisoned and they die. This, then, is the only way in which garden insecticides can safely be used indoors and even this is not recommended, nor, in fact, is it really necessary if you are looking after your plants correctly. The big plant nurseries take every precaution to ensure that our plants come to us clean and in good condition, and it is up to us to keep them that way.

The red spider mite

There are only three other pests which are at all common with the normal run of house-plants. You may come across one of your plants where the shoots are curling and twisting and changing colour, yet no greenfly or blackfly are present. The leaves affected will probably feel rough, dry and even brittle to the touch. This almost certainly indicates an attack by the unpleasant red spider mite, unpleasant because it is both difficult to detect and to clear. Even the name causes difficulties, for this mite is not a spider nor is it red. It makes fine, hairy, web-like secretions, mainly on the back of leaves and it can be identified for certain by looking for these. The mites themselves are almost invisible to the naked eye.

Red spider mite appears only when the atmosphere is too dry, that is to say when there is a dangerous lack of humidity. If your humidity levels are acceptable then your plants should never be attacked by this pest. So if you do find it the first thing to do is to increase the general level of humidity in the room that has been affected. The pest itself can be cleared by spraying thoroughly with an insecticide such as malathion, but only *outside* the house. If the attack is not severe it is worth while trying to clear it by spraying simply with clean water, making sure that every inch of the plant is drenched. It is possible to do this indoors if floor and furnishings are safely draped with newspaper.

Mealy bugs and others

It is possible also that when tending your plants you may see a curious white fluffy substance in one or two of the joints. It looks innocuous, almost as though a tiny feather or even a minute piece of cottonwool has been caught by the plant. But it will be mealy bug, a comparatively rare pest but one which is a nuisance for the only way to clear it on large plants is to pick it off by hand. If the white woolly blobs are examined closely you will find they contain one or more reddish mites and it is these that do the damage.

If the infestation is on a small plant it will be possible to take it outdoors

and, turning the pot upside down, dip the entire foliage of the plant into a bucket of a special solution of white oils by the name of VOLCK. This should clear the attack. But as it is usually the larger, older and hence more static plants that are involved, other methods are usually necessary. I use a VOLCK solution (made up quite simply according to directions) and a fine water-colour paint brush or sometimes a matchstick. The brush or the matchstick is dipped into the white oils and then the white fluff is carefully picked off the plant, every little piece of it. It can be a lengthy business if the plant is heavily infested but this should only be the case if it has been neglected or if it is in a room which is seldom used.

The last of these insect pests that we are at all likely to find is called scale, and it is a small insect in appearance something like a very small woodlouse except that it does not appear to move but remains stuck to a leaf surface, usually on the underside of the leaf, where it sucks at the sap. It is grey-green in colour and difficult to see unless you find one specimen and then specifically look for others.

This pest once again must be removed by hand and scraped with considerable effort from its limpet-like hold on the leaf surface. Alternatively it will be killed by the application of a systemic insecticide to the soil surface, but this will require several days to take effect while the plant can normally be cleared by hand in a matter of half an hour or so. It is probably the rarest of these very few common insect pests.

So we have seen that pests and diseases are nothing to frighten us. They are fewer, less important and infinitely less lethal than the pests and diseases we find in our gardens and we find to our shame that the greatest dangers facing house-plants are those brought by man.

It is a sad and curious fact that it is so frequently those who mean best, try hardest and wish most fervently for success with their house-plants who do them the greatest ill in the shortest possible time. I get many anxious, wistful, even frantic letters asking for advice and I bitterly regret that I cannot reply with definite recipes for success. It is quite impossible to tell a reader in, say, Sheffield, how many times she should water her *Fatshedera lizei* in her council house dining room, nor tell a reader in Eastbourne why her saintpaulia fails to bloom although she has apparently done everything absolutely according to the book.

GARDENS BEHIND GLASS

However, there is one way of gardening with house-plants that is about as foolproof as it can be, so simple in fact that many indoor gardeners think there must be a catch in it.

About 150 years ago a certain Dr Nathaniel Ward, an enthusiastic naturalist, wished to examine in detail the development of a chrysalis he had

Bottle gardens offer the indoor gardener a good opportunity for growing some of the more tender house plants. Choose those which are both small and slow-growing.

found in the woods, so he brought it home and packed it in a sealed glass jar with some soil from his garden. What happened to the chrysalis history has forgotten to tell us, but he found that certain seeds present in the soil germinated and lived as plants almost indefinitely without ever being watered, the same moisture being re-cycled indefinitely.

This might have remained a casual curiosity except for the fact that at about this time huge advances were being made by several plant hunters in the more remote parts of the world just being opened up. They discovered their new plants, they described them minutely in their notes and they drew the most meticulous representations of them, but seldom could they bring the plants back to this country safely, because of the terrible conditions and the lengthy period of the sea voyages involved.

Ward wondered if the principle he had noted could be applied to this problem. After much trial and error he produced a series of packing cases made from timber, cast iron and glass, in which the strange new plants could be inserted together with the moist soil in which they grew. These cases would then be carefully sealed and placed in the ships bound for home. Despite the length of the journeys, the salt spray which sometimes covered the cases and the lack of skilled attention to water the growing plants they survived and could be both examined and actually grown in places such as Kew Gardens when they reached England.

This was a great step forward for science and quickly enough some entrepreneur decided that the same principle might be adapted to the home. It was the time of the conservatory and also the time of gas lighting, smoky atmospheres, sealed windows, coal fires and other indoor plant perils. 'Wardian cases' were soon made, some of them quite attractive in a baroque kind of way, which enabled plants to be grown in the home safely and at length.

The principle is simple enough. In a sealed case the water cannot evaporate, so it is absorbed by the plant roots and breathed out by the plant foliage only to be condensed into moisture again to trickle down into the soil and be absorbed by the plant roots. It is a mystery why Wardian cases are not made or are not available today. I would have thought they would be eagerly sought and accepted by large numbers of people, particularly those who live in cities, in flats and apartments without gardens, and indeed by those who are ill or elderly.

Carboys and jars

Similar in principle to a Wardian case are bottle gardens and these have achieved tremendous popularity. These gardens are made in all kinds of bottles and other containers, glass jars, carboys, enormous brandy balloons and the like. There are several reasons for their success. The first is probably their curiosity or interest value. 'How did the plants get in there?' is the first question that is asked. Then, because the plants must necessarily be small and immature they have a certain endearing quality and look pretty and delicate. Thirdly there is no question that they last better this way; with an absolute minimum of attention and where conditions are poor, particularly with polluted atmospheres or those which are arid, the plants seem to have a good chance of a long and attractive life. These bottle gardens are not difficult to make, so long as a few basic principles are observed. The directions that follow for planting a carboy apply to any other kind of similar container. The first thing, of course, is to make quite sure that the container is uncracked and will not leak. It should then be meticulously cleaned both inside and out. One way of cleaning the interior is to put in some water and then a handful of sandy gravel. Swish this around thoroughly and then empty it away, using several fillings of water of gradually increasing heat, until you are left at the end with your carboy clean and hot. In this way the last few drops of water that might otherwise leave marks on the interior will evaporate in the heat.

Next, see to the absolutely vital drainage layer. This should be at least 1 in. deep and preferably twice that. It should consists of fine gravel, about pea-sized, and this should be poured very gently into the base. If you consider there is some risk of cracking the glass, then first make a thin carpet of peat and on top of this pour the gravel. Next add the soil. This should be just moist and fairly sharply drained. A John Innes mixture with added sharp sand will do, but make sure that you use the weakest mixture you can get—Potting No 1 is probably the ideal. The reason for this is that the plants we insert must be encouraged to grow as slowly as possible, otherwise they will quickly outgrow the limited amount of space available to them.

A more attractive layout can be achieved if the soil in the carboy is sloped rather than flat. This is easy enough to arrange, particularly if the soil is poured in through a cone or chute made from several layers of newspaper. This soil layer should not be less than about 2 in. deep anywhere and can go up to any depth that is attractive. It is a good plan, but by no means essential, to add on top of the basic layer of moist soil another, thinner layer of dry soil. The reason for this is that this dry top layer will act to some degree as a mulch and slow down evaporation. It will also make planting easier, for the roots of the tiny plants will go down into the moist soil and the drier layer can be easily pulled over.

Tools are a matter of improvisation. The best are a spoon to be used as a spade, a rammer for firming the soil around roots and a spiker to pick up and remove any dead leaves or similar debris. The spoon is easily enough strapped securely to a long cane. An excellent rammer is a cotton reel stuck and preferably glued into the base of a long, slim cane. The problem with the spiker is that it must spike efficiently. It is no use, for example, strapping a fork to the end of a cane for the prongs just are not sharp enough to penetrate, say, an ivy leaf lying on the surface of the soil. The best tool that I have found is a spiker made by strapping four or five long, sharp pins to the base of a cane so that they project for at least ½ in.

Plants to enclose in glass

Which plants to use? This is very much a matter of compromise, for what is wanted is a collection of plants that can be obtained in a small and immature state, that will grow slowly, that will not grow large, that will have roughly the same likes and dislikes in light, moisture and temperature, and of course that will look well. Although it is possible to buy collections of suitable plants as such, it is always more pleasant and more creative to choose your own. Do not try to get too many into the container; six or eight is usually quite enough. The following plants are all suitable and can usually be obtained small enough for a carboy.

Several of the codiaeums or crotons are small enough to use this way and they bring a welcome touch of colour, red, gold and white as well as green. The cryptanthus has one or two varieties which are suitable and they cover the soil closely as suggested by their popular names of earth star and starfish plant. *Fittonia verschaffeltii*, dainty, pink and silver, is better than *F. argyroneura*, which is sometimes temperamental when the weather turns cool. The hederas or ivies are normally too rampant for a bottle garden, *Hedera helix* Glacier and *H. h. lutzii* are both small-leaved, slow-growing and variegated. *Maranta leuconeura* and *M. makoyana* are two more beautiful plants, pale pink and chocolate, that are sometimes difficult to grow as specimens in the home but which tend to be much easier in a bottle garden. *Pellionia pulchra* is small, creeping, red, green and silver, very lovely.

Of the several peperomias the best for our purpose is probably the small, white and green, crinkled leaved *P. caperata variegata*. If you are able to trace a sample of *Sansevieria hahnii* this will give you a different shape, but its somewhat drab green and grey is better replaced with the golden variety. The pink and cream *Saxifraga sarmentosa tricolour* is a slow grower and several of the selaginellas are also sufficiently slow growing to qualify.

From this list it would be quite possible to select sufficient plants to make up a most attractive garden. Obviously the plants must be knocked from their pots before planting, but it will be helpful first to decide just where each is to go. Lay them out on a table so that you can see just how they will look together and then see to the planting.

Creating a 'jungle jar'

With your spoon dig a hole in the right place, being careful to get down into the moist compost. Then knock the plant from its pot and drop it through the aperture as near as possible to the right place. It is sometimes possible to lean the carboy or even to swing the plant by its foliage so that it falls in the hole prepared for it. Cover the roots with the spoon and then firm the soil around them with the rammer. Carry on in the same way with all the plants. Remember to keep the smallest or flattest growing of the plants on the lower slope of the 'hill' and the taller-growing plants towards the top. Contrast your colour and your texture to give greater interest.

When you have finished the planting you will probably find that you have left some traces of soil on the inner glass which spoils the look of the container. Tie a tissue to a piece of heavy gauge wire and see if you can bend this sufficiently to reach the offending spot. If this is impossible, you may be able to insert the nozzle of a spray and very lightly spray clean water on the spot until the dust or soil floats down to the soil level.

Do not water after planting, nor should you water again until it is obvious that some of the plants are in need of moisture. The best way to water then is to spray down through the top so that the plants have their leaves covered with a fine film of moisture. Do not give too much. In theory it should be possible to seal the carboy with a stopper or even with a rubber ball, but in practice it will be found that one or two of the plants will almost certainly damp off if this is done, so it is wiser to leave it open.

Stand the carboy where it gets good light but never sunlight, for this could generate such heat as to kill or burn some of the plants. Keep the interior meticulously clean. If a leaf falls make sure that it is removed as soon as possible. If one or two of the plants grow too quickly they can be pruned, sometimes with a pair of scissors or if too deep by fixing a razor blade onto a cane.

A planted carboy should last several years if it has been planted correctly and maintained carefully. By this time the plants will be filling the inside and creating the air of mystery that has earned this type of arrangement the name of 'jungle jars'. But it is unwise to let them grow too rampant, for the stronger plants will after a time strangle the weaker, to the detriment of the appearance of the container as a whole.

Gardens without soil

One of the major pleasures to be gained from a jungle jar or a planted bottle garden is to watch the plants grow over a long period. Another very simple method of gaining the same pleasure is to make one or two of what I call 'puddle pots', a very simple form of indoor gardening which I seem to have originated.

It consists of a waterproof container of any convenient shape or size, which is filled almost to the top with pebbles and water. The pebbles anchor little cuttings of suitable plants which grow in the water. If the right plants are chosen they grow well, although more slowly than in soil, so that one can plant a puddle pot and enjoy it for months. And at the same time, should one of the cuttings fail it can be removed very easily and another used to take its place. The water must be topped up regularly and if an occasional light feed is added the plants will benefit. After a time they may grow too large for the original puddle pot and will have to be removed, but by this time the roots will have grown sufficiently to allow it to be planted up to give you a new plant.

Any plant which can be rooted in water alone is a suitable candidate for the puddle pot. The list includes tradescantia, saxifraga, begonia, chlorophytum, scindapsus, *Philodendron scandens*, coleus, ivies, busy lizzies, and many more. You can use a single variety to a container or have them as mixed as you like.

The technique is really very simple. When the container has been chosen place a layer of pebbles on its floor and cover these with water. The size of the pebbles will depend on the size of the container, but I find in general that about 1 in. in diameter is best. If you have no pebbles, then you can use marbles, sea shells or anything else that will anchor your cuttings. Then take your cuttings and one by one place them in the container so that they can be anchored by further layers of pebbles to which water is added as the level rises.

If a cutting does not take, then the probability is that the stem base is clear of the water, so always make sure that the water level is kept topped up. An occasional, say monthly, application of a weak fertiliser solution will keep the plants growing away, but the intention is not to grow huge plants.

Plant collections for your friends

Puddle pots make lovely gifts and they have the advantage that they do not have to be planted up and grown on months ahead. If you are sure that the plants you have chosen as cuttings will grow easily and happily in water then there is little that can go wrong and you know also that your attractive gift can form the basis of a whole collection of pot plants, once the roots have grown sufficiently to allow them to be potted.

There are, in fact, many gifts one can make in this way. Somehow a mixture or collection of plants together in one container always seems to be both a more generous and a more personal gift than a single pot plant. A puddle pot is easy enough for the most inexperienced indoor gardener to handle and one of the benefits as well as the delights of several plants growing closely together in a single container is that they generally grow better this way. Each plant breathes out a certain amount of moisture through its leaves, so if several are growing closely together they are all spraying each other very gently with warm, moist air and providing the humidity for each other that they all need.

Groups of plants can be planted in a bowl directly into their soil, or as we have just seen in water and pebbles, or they can be left in their pots to grow separately, the actual plastic or terracotta pot being hidden by a covering layer of peat or some similar material. The benefit of the latter system is simply that it is easier to remove a pot and equally simple to replace it with another.

The arrangements can be as large as you like or as small, as lavish as you like or as simple, as colourful or as restrained. You can choose the container with special reference to a certain room colouring or period and you can decorate it for presentation with ribbon. You can use driftwood in your arrangement or you can incorporate various ornaments. For instance, you can make a little Japanese garden complete with miniature pagodas, temples, bridges and sampans.

There is really no limit to what you can create, once you are at home with your plants.

10 BULBS THROUGH THE YEAR

There is really nothing to growing flowers from bulbs these days because the merchants seem to make things easier and more foolproof all the time. A few years ago, when I was told that I could buy lily bulbs ready potted and that they would flower in about eight weeks with very little attention, I was doubtful, knowing that amateurs tend to have certain difficulties with lilies. But the bulbs lived up to the claim. And they were delightful. These lilies, a new hybrid called Harmony in this case, come already planted in containers together with complete instructions for their cultivation.

They are just one example of what are called 'prepared' bulbs. There are many more. Most people know about prepared hyacinths because they have been with us for a long time now. The bulbs are lifted as usual from the fields after they have been ripened and are then stored in special low-temperature chambers where the humidity is also controlled. This is done to accelerate the formation of the embryo flower bud. But where you can keep untreated bulbs waiting a little while until it is convenient to give the time to planting them, these prepared bulbs should be planted immediately they are received.

Most people order prepared hyacinths because they wish to have them in flower for Christmas. If they follow the planting instructions which the merchant sends with the bulbs they are almost certain to get them to bloom at that time.

The Roman hyacinth

However, there are other little hyacinths which will bloom early quite naturally. Of these the white Roman hyacinth is perhaps the best known. Their bulbs are very small. The flowers are nothing like the opulent spikes of the other kinds of hyacinths, but on the other hand more than one is produced from each bulb. They are dainty enough to be planted with table decorations in mind. The method of growing them is simplicity itself, because they can even be grown in pebbles and water (I use well-washed shingle) with the water level just below the bases of the bulbs. If they actually sit in water the flower spikes will be stunted when they grow. They can also be planted in bulb fibre or in any of the potting composts.

Like most other spring-flowering bulbs they should be grown in the cool and the dark until the roots are strong and firm, when they can be brought out into the light. As Roman hyacinths are early types this will mean about the beginning of November. Do not be in a hurry to bring any bulbs into heat. They need to mature slowly. A temperature of about 50°F (10°C) will do for the Roman hyacinths. Once the flowers look near to opening you can bring them into a warm room. Do remember that the warmer the atmosphere into which you bring them the shorter their lives will be. Keep them watered, but only moderately.

If you think of Roman hyacinths in terms of flower arrangement, although they are actually growing you can plant them in such a way that you can dispense with some cut flowers while they are in bloom. Prepare for plant arrangements well ahead. When you are filling the bowl lower an empty flower pot into the centre, or even more than one if you are planting a large bowl. Let it stay there while the roots of the bulbs are growing, for they will by-pass it neatly. When you finally bring the bowl out into the open have

Below: *Crocus chrysanthus* varieties will bloom for Christmas so long as they are potted early in the autumn.

Right: Colchicum or meadow saffron bulbs will flower even though they are not planted in soil or growing in water.

ready a plant, a variegated ivy or a good specimen of tradescantia, for example. Take out the empty flower pot and replace it with the plant. This will mean that while waiting for the hyacinth blooms to appear your bowl will have interest and colour. Alternatively you can 'plant' a container full of water and when the time comes fill this with an early spring mixture, ivy trails and berries, winter flowering jasmine, snippets of early blossom such as viburnum, or perhaps even a separate flowering plant such as a little azalea or a cyclamen.

There are some early varieties of hyacinths which can be grown in exactly the same way as the Romans. These are coloured pink, blue and rose. All are delightfully fragrant. If you like the more delicate types of hyacinths try the Cynthella varieties. There is a really wide range of colours in these. They will flower from the middle of January onwards. And incidentally, a mixture of these planted outdoors will give you some lovely flowers for cutting later in the spring.

Lily of the valley

Like the true lilies referred to earlier, lily of the valley (botanically convallaria and not a lily) can also be bought as a packaged deal. These will flower in three weeks exactly from the time they are despatched by the supplier. These are also ready planted, usually ten 'crowns' to a pot. Naturally you can mass several pots in one container for a splendid arrangement. But I suggest that when you take your Roman hyacinths out of the dark you plant a pot of lily of the valley in the centre instead of, or as well as, another kind of plant. This way you will have a really fragrant spring-like group in the darkest days of winter.

Alternatively, instead of the packaged deal you can buy specially prepared crowns and pot the lily of the valley yourself. These are perhaps a little more trouble. In this case they have to be planted immediately they are received in peat, leaf mould, a standard potting compost or even in sand. In any case the medium must be kept constantly moist. They must grow in a temperature of 50–55°F (10–13°C) in a moist but dark place. You can grow them under the sink but you would have to keep spraying the air unless you covered the plants in some way. A good method is to put the pot inside a black plastic bag and fasten this at the top. Peep into it from time to time and when the leaves are 3–4 in. high bring the pot out into the full light. Keep it watered of course.

When one considers how simple it is to grow some kinds of bulbs, it really does seem to be making heavy weather of it to go to all the traditional business of potting certain kinds, plunging them out of doors in deep ashes and so on. This is an ideal method for those who need a hobby but there are several easier ways.

Bulbs to grow in water

Take the 'puddle lovers' for instance. There are several kinds which, like the Roman hyacinths, will grow in nothing but pebbles and water, with just a little charcoal in among the stones to keep the water sweet. Some of the prettiest of these are the polyanthus or bunch-flowered narcissi. If you so wish you can order specially treated bulbs so that they will flower in time for Christmas, in which case you will have to follow the directions faithfully.

For any kind, prepared or not, use rain water if possible and deep bowls. Put pebbles in these to within about 2 in. of the rims. Place as many bulbs in each bowl as you like, so long as they do not actually touch each other. Wedge them upright if necessary with a pebble or two. The water should come just below the bulb bases, not actually touching them. The bowls must then be placed in a cool place, but this time it is not so important that it is completely dark, although the bulbs always seem to grow better when they have been in the dark. An easy way of providing darkness is simply to make a kind of cone of dark or thick paper and place this over the bowl. There are other types of narcissi, which include daffodils, which can be grown this way.

They must be kept cool, with temperatures no higher than 45°F (7°C). By the end of November they can come into warmer temperatures, though still cooler than normal living room warmth. Grow them on a window-sill in good light so long as this is not over a radiator. The growing plants should not be coddled.

There are some bulbs easier to grow. Colchicum or meadow saffron for example, sometimes wrongly called autumn crocus. These have so much nourishment packed into their great fat bulbs that they will grow without soil or even without water. All you have to do is stand the bulbs in a low bowl or something of the kind and wait for the flowers. The bulbs are on sale in late summer and the flowers appear in autumn. For a memorable decoration buy several and fill a bowl.

Crocuses and tulips

The spring crocuses generally are a little more tricky to grow indoors. Failure usually lies in bringing them in too soon, they must spend the early part of their sojourn in bowls or pots out of doors. They should not be brought in until the buds are almost ready to open. However, *Crocus vernus* Vanguard will bloom for Christmas so long as it is potted early. *Crocus crysanthus* varieties also are good and early for indoor decoration. The large Dutch varieties can be disappointing and in their case white and purple varieties force but yellow ones will not do so well. I have grown the former quite well in pebbles and water.

Not all tulips force well but there are a few which do and generally speaking they need careful cultivation. They should be planted in soil and pots should be plunged out of doors. Timing when they are brought indoors is also important. The double tulips are attractive, a little like full blown roses and some are unexpectedly fragrant. Do not mix varieties in one bowl and this goes for all bulbs. You will get uneven growth if you do.

You can also buy just a few varieties of early tulips which are specially prepared to flower for Christmas. These are mainly reds except for one or two yellows, ideal colours for the season. Once again if you want you can plan ahead for mixed arrangements, introducing empty vessels or pots around which the roots will grow. This is a much better way than lifting flowering bulbs from boxes and making mixed arrangements, for inevitably some root damage is caused this way. It is most important that you do not try to hurry tulips into flower. Let them grow slowly and in a maximum temperature of some 65–70°F (18–21°C) and always in good light once they have been brought out from the dark.

The exciting 'amaryllis'

Probably no other bulbs are so exciting to grow as those called amaryllis by the bulb merchant and hippeastrum by the true plantsman. (Amaryllis, strictly, are belladonna lilies which grow outdoors and flower in the autumn.) Like so many other bulbs these too can be bought prepared to flower by Christmas day. Otherwise they are not even potted until January or February. Sometimes specially treated bulbs are on sale in summer for autumn flowering.

There is one point about hippeastrums which differentiates them from most other bulbs: they respond to bottom heat. This means that they can be grown on a sunny window-sill over a radiator, so long as watering is not forgotten and you can provide a little extra humidity near the plant.

When they are potted half the bulb, the 'nose', should be above the soil. They must have a well-drained potting compost and it is wise to mix this with a good proportion of clean silver sand if you have any doubts about its porosity. One bulb merchant recommends that you soak the lower part of the new bulb and its roots in tepid water for about five days before potting it. Pots should not be too large, just wide enough to allow about 1 in. of soil all around the bulb. Give it just a little water at first, then water it freely once growth begins. The pot should never stand in water.

Lilies and little orchids

Prepared or treated lily bulbs can be bought which when planted in December will flower in February or March. Many kinds of untreated lily bulbs will

Hippeastrum, popularly known as amaryllis is so easy to grow and extremely rewarding. The beautiful caladium and the canary ivy are in separate pots.

grow well in pots. Failure lies in keeping them too warm in the early stages. They should be in a cool place at about 50°F (10°C). Here the soil should be kept moist but not wet. Alternatively the pots can be plunged in the garden and covered with 2 in. of peat or bracken. Once the shoots come through and are about 3 in. high the pots can be brought into a frame, a cool greenhouse or a window-sill in a cool part of the house. Not until the buds are really fully formed should the plants be brought into heat. They must be shaded from the sun. You need good pots, 6 in. in diameter and more if you are growing several bulbs to a pot. The tips of the bulbs should be about $1\frac{1}{2}$ in. beneath the soil surface.

There are many plants which will grow the year through from bulbs. Some need not go out into the garden after they have flowered but need to be rested and ripened after flowering, like the hippeastrum. These include

Some of the hardy, rock garden orchids make charming windowsill plants. They are easily grown from bulbs. This species, shown here with pelargoniums, is Bletilla.

nerines, veltheimia, eucomis, haemanthus, hymenocallis, sprekelia and oxalis. Clivias are handsome plants though large and they do not need to die down in the same way.

If you like fragrant flowers grow *Acidanthera murielae.* Plant the corms in late March to early May, five corms to a 6 in. pot. Keep them on a window-sill in a warm room or in a greenhouse. Water freely as the corms grow vigorously and just a little at other times. Dry them off when they fade.

In the bulb merchants' catalogues you will usually find bulbs, corms, tubers, crowns and pseudo-bulbs all grouped and classified as bulbs, purely for the sake of convenience. Not strictly a bulb but sold as such is the charming little window-sill orchid bletilla. These also are treated and often sold packaged. They are charming flowers and so easy to grow. I bought the loose, not packaged 'bulbs' and planted six together in one shallow bowl in one of the soil-less composts. I found they needed plenty of water during their peak growing period; planted in March, they flowered in May. The sprays of little orchids took a long time to open which was pleasing, for the individual blooms did not last many days. Bletilla can be planted from December onwards. They can be grown outdoors in a sheltered rock garden.

Reviving after a rest: All spring bulbs and lilies including convallaria which have been forced into early bloom can be planted in the garden as soon as the weather permits. They will take two or three years perhaps to make up the vigour they have lost through being forced but they will flower again one day. Hyacinths never produce such large blooms again, but the smaller flowers are delightful and very graceful for arrangements.

A browse through a bulb or seed catalogue can be very rewarding because you can find many lovely plants which can be grown from tubers such as begonias, those with the great rose-like flowers. You have to start the tubers in February or March in peat or leaf mould in a temperature of about 65–70°F (18–21°C). Transfer them to larger pots as necessary. Water moderately at first, freely later. Feed with liquid plant food when the buds begin to form. Shade the plants from sun and after they have flowered give the tubers a resting period.

Gloxinias need much the same treatment except that they are best either watered from below or plunged in moist peat.

11 ABC OF REWARDING INDOOR PLANTS

The following list does not pretend to be complete, for almost any plant can be grown indoors for certain periods. It includes those plants which are easily obtained and indicates those which are easily grown under normal home conditions and those which are slightly more pernickety. All return moderate attention with a wealth of beauty, interest, value and long life. The list is alphabetical and where possible the common or popular names are mentioned as well as the botanical, so that there should be no difficulty in tracing any particular plant.

Adiantum *cuneatum* (maidenhair fern): Difficult to grow except in a warm, humid atmosphere with clean air and no draughts. But worth trying.

Aechmea *rhodocyanea* (Greek vase plant): An easy to grow, delightful and long-lived bromeliad. It has grey-green strap-like leaves arching from a central 'vase' which should always be kept topped up with water and from which rises the tall pink scape, or flower stem, bearing the beautiful pink, blue and violet flowers.

African violet, see **Saintpaulia** *ionantha*

Aglaonema: There are several of these aroids, generally similar in appearance with green spear-shaped leaves splashed, flecked or striped with grey or silver. Easy to grow.

Ananas *comosus* (pineapple): Beautiful, spiky plants frequently with variegated gold and green leaves, these are easy to grow and long-lived. Plain green ones can be grown from the tuft at the top of a pineapple.

Anthurium: There are two or three of these, usually *A. andreanum* and *A. scherzerianum*, usually known as the palette plant, the piggy tail plant or the flamingo flower. Their main characteristic is the red, pink or white 'palette' flower from which rises the creamy-white 'piggy tail', almost straight in *andreanum* and usually curled in *scherzerianum*. Foliage is a glossy green.

Aphelandra *squarrosa louisae* (zebra plant or saffron spike): So named because

One of many lovely *Begonia rex* varieties is this Turnford Hall, a particularly 'house-hardy' plant. Begonias should not be stood in direct sunlight.

of the heavy white stripes on the leaves and the bright yellow cockscomb of a flower. Not really an easy plant to grow for long periods, but more recent varieties are tougher and easier.

Araucaria *excelsa* (Norfolk island pine): A tough and tiny pine which will even grow outdoors in mild areas. Grey-green foliage in regular branches. Easy.

Aspidistra *elatior* (parlour palm or cast iron plant): The popular names derive from the fact that it used to be seen in every parlour and seems to withstand almost any treatment. But it takes a long time to grow and is now in short supply. Even more attractive is the variegated type with golden or creamy striped leaves.

Azalea *indica:* A popular flowering house plant, particularly around Christmas, when it is a mass of white, pink, red or brick-coloured flowers. The root ball has usually been trimmed to get the plant into a small pot, so it is highly sensitive to drought. Keep the soil moist at all times. Look for the base of the main trunk; this should show up as wet and dark brown. If it looks dry, or the same brown as the upper portions, then the plant needs water badly.

Begonia: Many types, flowering and foliage, all of them beautiful, most fairly easy. (See opposite.)

Beloperone *guttata* (shrimp plant): So called because of the brownish-pink bracts and flowers it produces through most of the year. Give maximum light and feed regularly.

Busy Lizzie, see **Impatiens** *sultanii*

Cast iron plant, see **Aspidistra** *elatior*

Chlorophytum *comosum variegatum* (spider plant): This plant gets its name from the way in which the long, yellow and green striped narrow leaves branch out from the centre. An easy plant which produces long, arching stems bearing at the ends new baby plants which will root easily if placed in soil.

Christmas cactus, see **Zygocactus** *truncatus*

Cineraria *cruentis:* A familiar and endearing flowering plant with many-coloured, daisy-like flowers. Easy to grow indoors for short periods, but inclined to attract and harbour greenfly. Best watered with a systemic insecticide before being brought indoors.

Cissus *antarctica* (kangaroo vine): One of the best of the climbers. It will live almost for ever without special treatment and can be trained to cover a wall, climb a pole or form a room divider.

Citrus *mitis:* A miniature orange tree which will carry sweetly-scented flowers and tiny fruits at the same time. Keep moist at all times and comparatively humid. Brush the flowers lightly with a soft brush to assist fertilisation and increase the fruit yield.

Codiaeum *variegatum pictum* (croton): This plant can be most beautiful, with its gold and cream and red and green flecked leaves, but until recently it demanded more humid conditions than we were prepared to offer it indoors. New cultivars are tougher, more adaptable, and they seem to be getting better all the time.

Coleus *blumei* hybrids: These magnificently coloured plants are easy to grow from seed and from cuttings; they can be as vivid as flowers and they can last for months. Keep moist at the roots and if possible with some humidity.

Columnea *banksii*: A splendid and too little known trailing plant with glossy green leaves and vivid scarlet trumpet-shaped flowers which appear in winter. Place it high so it can trail and give it plenty of light.

Croton, see **Codiaeum**

Crown of thorns, see **Euphorbia** *bojeri.*

Some cyclamen, known as Rex strain, are decorative even when not in flower. Near this plant are narcissi growing in pebbles and a bowl of mixed ivy, peperomia and cryptanthus.

Cryptanthus (earth star or starfish plant): Several varieties exist of this attractive and low-growing bromeliad which forms a spreading rosette. Keep the central 'vase' filled with water, but otherwise they need little or no special attention. (See pages 120–121.)

Cyclamen *persicum:* These familiar hybrids decorate many homes during winter and seldom last as long as they should because they are kept too warm.

A beautiful new variety of dracaena, Rededge, with *Peperomia glabella* and with gynura.

They like cool conditions and should never be allowed to dry out.

Dieffenbachia (dumb cane): The popular name for this plant and its several varieties is given because if any of the sap reaches the mouth it will cause intense pain and swelling. All parts of the plant are poisonous, so beware. It has large spear-shaped leaves attractively flecked, blotched and striped with cream or white.

Dracaena:-There are a number of dracaenas, all distinguished for their beautiful foliage but otherwise differing fairly widely. They are all comparatively easy to grow. (See page 147.)

Dumb cane, see **Dieffenbachia**

Earth star, see **Cryptanthus**

Euphorbia *bojeri* (crown of thorns): The popular name derives from the wickedly long and sharp thorns and the tiny scarlet 'blood drop' flowers. This is a curiously attractive plant which will live for many years (my own is about 20 years old) without growing too large or demanding much attention.

Euphorbia *pulcherrima* (poinsettia): This is another member of the euphorbia family but entirely different. The white or pink are less striking than the vivid scarlet but equally attractive. The latest varieties are so strong that they will last for many months and can be brought into colour again after a brief autumn rest.

Fatshedera *lizei:* A curious hybrid resulting from a cross between the fatsia and the hedera. It is an attractive plant with large palmate leaves, usually grown trained up a stem but capable of growing as a sprawler. Easy to grow.

Ficus: A large family of house-plants which includes the well-known rubber plant and similar tree-like specimens as well as creeping, trailing and sprawling kinds. Most are comparatively easy to grow, all are distinctive and worth while. (See opposite.)

Fittonia *argyroneura* (snake skin plant): This gets its name from the beautiful silvery veins etched on the surface of the many leaves. A small plant and rather delicate but so beautiful that it is worth growing even if its life is short. Give it warmth, humidity and protection.

Geranium, see **Pelargonium**

Goldfish plant, see **Hypocyrta** *glabra*

Goose foot plant, see **Syngonium** *podophyllum*

Grape ivy, see **Rhoicissus** *rhomboidea*

Three types of ficus demonstrate the difference in the species, the large-leaved *F. decora* or rubber plant, *F. benjamina,* and the trailing *F. pumila.*

Greek vase plant, see **Aechmea** *rhodocyanea*

Hedera (ivy): There are so many varieties and cultivars here that it is impossible to list them all. They differ in the size and shape of the leaves, in their coloration and in their habit of growth. They are all easy to grow, undemanding of attention and will live almost for ever. (See page 146.)

Hippeastrum hybrids: These bulb flowers, sometimes known as amaryllis,

Maranta or the peacock plant likes a little constant humidity. This is easily and attractively provided if the plant is sunk into peat kept moist but not sodden.

Monstera deliciosa: the description refers to the fruit (unlikely, except in a green-house) but its foliage makes it an extremely handsome indoor plant.

produce huge, dramatic and vividly coloured flowers with the minimum of attention. Usual flowering time is winter and early spring. The bulbs can, of course, be dried off and grown again next year. (See page 140.)

Hoya *carnosa variegata:* Although known popularly as the wax flower, this variety is unlikely to produce the dainty white blooms which appear more regularly on *H. bella*. But this twining climber is known instead for the pretty, chunky white-edged leaves which seem to appear almost miraculously from the apparently naked long and probing shoots.

Hypocyrta *glabra* (goldfish plant): So named because of the little orange-red flowers. It is easy to grow and tolerant of poor conditions.

Impatiens *sultanii* (busy Lizzie): This very popular plant grows easily, flowering readily. Latest varieties have added new colours.

Kangaroo vine, see **Cissus** *antarctica*

Maidenhair fern, see **Adiantum** *cuneatum*

Maranta *makoyana* (peacock plant): The name derives from the flaunted beauty of the foliage, two-toned pink with chocolate markings. This is not an easy plant to grow for long periods and seems to do best in a bowl with other plants. (See page 150.)

Monstera *deliciosa* (Swiss cheese plant): So named because of the holes in the large and beautiful leaves; 'delicious' refers to the fruit, unlikely here except in a greenhouse, which tastes like a cross between pineapple and banana. Any easy aroid, the monstera will grow very large indeed. (See page 151.)

Mother-in-law's tongue, see **Sansevieria** *trifasciata laurentii*

Mother of thousands, see **Saxifraga** *stolonifera*

Neoregelia: Sometimes sold under different names, this is another of the excellent bromeliads which are so attractive and so easy to grow as house-plants. This, again, grows as a rosette having a central 'vase' which should be kept topped up with water at all times.

Nertera *depressa:* A charming, tiny, ground-covering creeping herb, covered with vivid, shining orange berries. It is easy to grow and will even grow outdoors in some sheltered districts. It likes some moisture and warmth, not too much direct sun.

Nidularium *marechati:* Still another bromeliad of roughly the same shape, size and habits as the others; blushes a deep scarlet when it is about to give birth to its flowers.

Norfolk Island pine, see **Araucaria** *excelsa*

Palette plant, see **Anthurium**

Parlour palm, see **Aspidistra** *elatior*

Peacock plant, see **Maranta** *makoyana*

Pelargonium: Sometimes wrongly called geranium, this splendid family gives us several types of plants, all beautiful, generous with vivid foliage or with brilliant and long lasting flowers. Will grow outdoors in summer and all through the winter if protected.

Pellionia *pulchra:* A little-known but charming small creeping plant with delicate silver, red and green leaves. Slow growing.

Peperomia: There are several of these, all attractive and useful, for they differ widely in leaf shape and colour but grow well and easily. *P. caperata variegata* has small cream and green crinkled leaves. *P. magnoliaefolia variegata* is larger, chunkier, glossier and smoother. *P. obtusifolia* has thick, fleshy leaves, dark green with a purple edge. (See page 147.)

Platycerium, one of the easiest of ferns to grow indoors, will live for years, given moderate care.

Philodendron: This large family of aroids includes about a dozen varieties for the home, most of them climbers or sprawlers, mostly fairly large and all of them easy and attractive. (See page 113.)

Piggy tail plant, see **Anthurium**

Platycerium *alicorne* (Stag's horn fern): So called from its forked or branching shape and slightly furry texture. Easy to grow and very attractive, it will live for years given moderate care. (See page 153.)

Plectranthus *fruticosus:* This attractive little plant with its glossy round leaves grows under almost all conditions quickly and easily. It will even grow in water alone; cuttings start to take root almost before they are severed from the plant.

Poinsettia, see **Euphorbia** *pulcherrima*

Rhoicissus *rhomboidea* (Grape ivy): An easy climber which will grow almost anywhere indoors, live for years, cover a wall and look attractive at all times.

Rubber plant, see **Ficus**

Saffron spike, see **Aphelandra** *squarrosa louisae*

Saintpaulia *ionantha* (African violet): This dainty little flowering plant, which has nothing to do with violets, can be kept in flower the whole year through, once you get it to feel at home with you. Yet many plant-lovers find it refuses to flower or even to flourish for them. Clean air and good light are essential.

Sansevieria *trifasciata laurentii* (Mother-in-law's tongue): So named because it is sharp and pointed but at the same time easy, tolerant, valuable and standing up well to neglect and mistreatment! Attractive and useful because of its characteristic shape. (See page 112; also shown on cover.)

Saxifraga *stolonifera* (Mother of thousands): This plant has an endearing habit of putting out dozens of hair-like stolons each bearing at the end a tiny baby plantlet. Easy to grow, attractive in shape and colour, but so prolific that it ages quickly. The tiny plantlets grow quickly if merely rested on the soil of another pot, so renew your stock regularly.

Scindapsus *aureus:* Available in several forms, the scindapsus is an attractive climber with gold-flecked and marbled heart-shaped leaves. The differences in the varieties are in leaf size and coloration. Fairly easy to grow, needing plenty of light.

Shrimp plant, see **Beloperone** *guttata*

Snake skin plant, see **Fittonia** *argyroneura*

Solanum *capsicastrum* (winter cherry): A Christmas gift plant bearing vivid orange or scarlet berries. A difficult plant to keep, especially in convivial atmospheres.

Sonerila *margaritacea:* The dark green leaves of this attractive plant are covered with silvery dots. It likes warm, draught-free conditions but dislikes direct sunlight. Water freely from early summer to autumn. (See above.)

Stag's horn fern, see **Platycerium** *alicorne*

Syngonium *podophyllum* (goose foot): So called because its large leaves

Sonerila margaritacea is a comparative newcomer to the home. A native of Java, it needs warmth, plenty of water and shade.

resemble the arrow-shaped foot of a goose. They are lobed with a central lobe and a number of side lobes. This plant produces aerial roots and needs bark or some other support for these. It will take large quantities of water as the days lengthen and will benefit from spraying on hot days.

Tradescantia *fluminensis* (wandering Jew or wandering sailor): Presumably so named because it grows so quickly and travels so far. Seldom seen at its best, for it needs pinching out before the trails grow too long. Light feeds help enormously. This is one of the few house-plants which is taken so much for granted that it too often goes unwatered and unfed for long periods.

Wandering Jew, Wandering sailor, see **Tradescantia** *fluminensis*

Wax flower, see **Hoya** *carnosa variegata*

Winter cherry, see **Solanum** *capsicastrum*

Zebra plant, see **Aphelandra** *squarrosa louisae*

Zebrina *pendula:* Like the tradescantia in appearance but slightly larger, fleshier and more vividly coloured.

Zygocactus *truncatus:* Christmas cactus, although it does not flower automatically at that time but depends both on the season and the treatment it receives. Opulent pink, white or red flowers are produced from the ends of the claw-like joints of its flat stems, which resemble leaves.

INDEX

(Picture page references are shown in bold type)

Abstract arrangements, *35*
Acacia, *52*
Acidanthera, *142*
Acroclinium, *55,* **56, 161**
Adiantum cuneatum (maidenhair fern), *143*
Aechmea rhodocyanea (Greek vase plant), *108, 114, 143*
African violet, see *Saintpaulia ionantha*
Aglaonema, *143*
Aira, *91*
Alchemilla, *82, 86, 91*
Alligator pear, **60,** *62*
'All-round' arrangements, **15,** *16–9,* **18,** *70*
'Amaryllis', see Hippeastrum
Ananas comosus (pineapple), *143*
Anthurium, *143*
Aphelandra squarrosa louisae (zebra plant or saffron spike), *108, 143–5*
Aphid, *126–7*
Apple, **23,** *37, 42, 73, 76, 100*
Araucaria excelsa (Norfolk island pine), *114, 116, 145*
Artichoke, *77, 79, 83*
Arum, *91, 103*
Aspidistra, *114, 116, 145*
Asymmetrical arrangements, *34–5*
Atriplex (mountain spinach), *85*
Aubergine, *95, 100*
Autumn, **25,** *26, 54, 58, 75, 83, 86, 90, 92, 136*
Azalea, *108, 137*; *indica, 145*

Bark, *76, 81, 102*
Barley, *55,* **67,** *80, 98*
Beech, *12, 19, 34, 58–9, 73*
Begonia, **100, 105,** *108, 133, 142,* **144,** *145*
Beloperone guttata (shrimp plant), *145*
Bergenia, *82, 86*
Blackberry, *100*
Blackfly, see Aphid
Bletilla, *142*
Blossom, *11, 22, 34, 39, 42, 45, 52, 80, 82, 83, 87, 97, 137*
Bluebell, *58*
Bottle gardens, *130–3*
Box (tree), *58, 74*
Bracken, *62,* **67,** *80, 141*
Brassica, *83*
Briza (quaking grass), *55, 91*
Broccoli, *83*
Bromus (false oats), *55, 67*
Brussels sprouts, *83*
Bulrush, *56*
Busy Lizzie, see *Impatiens sultanii*
Byzantine cone, **15,** *16, 80*

Cabbage, *35,* **73,** *83,* **85,** *95*
Cactus, *106,* **109**
Caladium, **140**
Camellia, *58–9,* **75**
Canary creeper, **40**
Candles, candlesticks, *43, 70,* **73,** *81*
Candytuft, *37*
Carboys, *130–3*
Cardoon, *79, 83*
Carnation, *62, 93, 95, 100, 103*
Catkins, **77, 78,** *80, 83, 87*
Centaurea candidissima, 83
Central heating, *53, 110*
Chicory, **25**
Chincherinchee, *100*
Chinese lantern, see Physalis
Chlorophytum comosum variegatum (spider plant), *114, 133, 145*

Christmas, *16, 20, 21, 37, 43, 48, 52, 66–73,* **68–9, 72,** *81, 83, 92, 102, 135,* **136,** *138, 139*; cactus, see *Zygocactus truncatus*; rose, *86, 90*
Chrysanthemum, **33,** *62,* **65, 73,** *93, 98, 99,* **116**
Cineraria cruentis, 145; maritimis, 83
Cissus antarctica (kangaroo vine), *114, 145*
Citrus mitis, 145–6
Clary, *85*
Codiaeum, *132*; *variegatum pictum* (croton), *146*
Coix lacryma-jobi, 91
Colchicum, **136–7,** *139*
Coleus, *133*; *blumei, 146*
Colour, *35–7, 42–3, 50, 103*
Columbine, **84**
Cones, conifers, *59–62,* **60,** *66, 68, 70,* **71,** *73–4*
Containers, *11–2, 19, 21 2, 27 9, 34 5, 38–52, 63, 80–1*; glass, *34, 42–3,* **47,** *48–50,* **49,** *52, 81, 129–33*; metal, *12,* **25, 40–1,** *42, 43,* **44,** *62, 63, 81, 103*; waterproofing, **40**; wooden, *12, 81*
Copper beech, *59*
Coral, *98*
Cork, *76, 81, 102*
Cornus mas, **46**
Cortaderia (pampas grass), *55, 79*
Crab apple, *73*
Crescent arrangements, *27, 73–4*
Crocus, **77, 136,** *138*; 'autumn', see Colchicum
Croton, see *Codiaeum variegatum pictum*
Crown of thorns, see *Euphorbia bojeri*
Cryptanthus (earth star or starfish plant), *62, 102–3,* **120–1,** *132,* **146,** *147*
Cycas leaves, *64,* **67,** *79*
Cyclamen, *110, 114,* **116,** *137,* **146,** *147–8*

Daffodil, *27, 42, 80, 87, 95, 97, 98*
Dahlia, **25,** *42, 62, 99, 100, 103*
Daisy, **17,** *34, 54, 80,* **88,** *98–9*
Dandelion, *9,* **20**
Delphinium, **17,** *59*
Dianthus, **85**
Dieffenbachia (dumb cane), *148*
Disease, *108, 115, 126–9*
'Double leg', **75,** *76–7, 79*
Dracaena, **147,** *148*
Dried flowers and plants, **44,** *53–63,* **56, 57, 61,** *80, 82–3, 87, 95, 98*
Driftwood, *50, 62, 95,* **101,** *102, 103–6, 134*
Dumb cane, see Dieffenbachia
'Dusty Millers', *83*

Earth star, see Cryptanthus
Easter, **77, 78,** *80–1*
Eggs, **78,** *80–1*
Elaeagnus, *58, 70, 87*
Escalonia, **25**
Eucalyptus, *58–9, 95–7*
Euphorbia, *52, 79, 85–6*; *bojeri* (crown of thorns), *108, 148*; *epithymoides, 86*; *heterophylla* (Mexican fire flower), *85*; *marginata, 85*; *pilosa major, 86*; *pulcherrima* (poinsettia), *79, 148*
Evergreens, *34, 43, 52, 58–9, 66,* **71,** *74, 75, 79, 83, 86, 87*
Everlasting flowers, *53–63*

'Faced' arrangements, *19–20*
Fatshedera lizei, 114, 129, 148
Feeding, *52, 112–3, 119, 122, 133–4*
Fennel, *92*
Fern, *10, 12, 19, 59, 64, 70, 80*
Ficus, *114, 122, 124, 148,* **149**
Fittonia argyroneura (snake skin plant), *132*; *verschaffeltii, 132*
Floral balls, *66*
FLORAPAK foamed plastic, *49, 110*
Flowering currant, *87*
Foamed plastic, *39,* **40,** *41, 43, 49, 52, 54–5, 62–6, 68, 70, 74, 75, 76,* **78,** *80, 81, 98, 99, 103*
Foil, *39,* **40,** *62, 74, 81*
Forget-me-not, **65**
Formaldehyde, *52*
Freesia, *42, 95, 97,* **100,** *103*
Frosting and glitter, *64, 67–8, 74, 79, 83, 92*
Fuchsia, *37,* **40**
Fungi, *11, 53*

Garlands, *48, 73–5*
Garrya elliptica, 87
Gas, *118*
Gentian, **17**
Geranium, see Pelargonium
Gladiolus, *38, 59, 90, 93, 97–8, 103,* **105**
Gloxinia, *142*
Glycerine, *58, 87, 98*
Gnaphalium, **44**
Godetia, *99*
Golden rod, **25,** *59*
Goldfish plant, see *Hypocyrta glabra*
Goose foot plant, see *Syngonium podophyllum*
Gourd, **60,** *62, 76*
Grapes, **24,** *26, 76, 100*
Grape ivy, see *Rhoicissus rhomboidea*
Grasses, *11, 12, 19, 55, 63, 64, 67, 82,* **88,** *91, 98*
Greek vase plant, see *Aechmea rhodocyanea*
Greenfly, see Aphid
Greenhouse, *13, 102, 122, 141, 142,* **151**

Grevillea (silk oak), *58, 97,* **101**
Guelder rose, **33**
Gynura, **147**
Gypsophila, **40,** *59*

Hare's tail, *55, 91*
Harvest arrangements, *75–6*
Heather, **47**
Hedera (ivy), *42,* **46, 47,** *79, 80,* **94,** *95,* **100,** *100–2, 114–6, 119, 132, 133, 136,* **140, 146,** *150*
Helichrysum (strawdaisy), **44,** *54,* **56, 61,** *66, 70, 73, 80, 83,* **94**
Hellebore, *86, 90*
Henbane, **57**
Hippeastrum, **24,** *26, 139–40,* **140,** *141, 150–2*
'Hogarth curve', see 'Lazy S'
Holly, *37, 42, 66, 70,* **71**
Honesty, *59, 64,* **68–9, 84**
Hordeum jubatum, 91
Hosta, *82–4*
Hoya, *152*
Humidity, *52, 53, 110–1, 114, 118, 127, 135, 140,* **150**: see also Water
Hyacinth, *114, 135–8, 142*; roman, **77,** *135–8*
Hydrangea, **17, 44,** *59*
Hypocyrta glabra (goldfish plant), *152*

Ikebana, 30–2, 39
Impatiens sultanii (Busy Lizzie), *133, 152*
Iris, *42, 59, 90*
Ivy, see Hedera

Japan, Japanese terms, *10, 11, 14,* **28,** *29–32, 35, 134*
Jasmine, *137*
Job's tears, see *Coix lacryma-jobi*
'Jungle jars', *130–3*

Kale, **47,** *70–3, 83,* **85, 104**
Kangaroo vine, see *Cissus antarctica*
Kubari, 50, **51**
Larch, *35, 59–61*
Laurel, *58–9*
'Lazy S', **33,** *34–5, 41*
Leek, **84**
Lichen, *11, 59*
Light, *108–9, 115–6,* **116, 117,** *118–9, 122, 133, 135–6, 138–9,* **144, 155**
Ligularia, **57**
Lily, *55, 103, 135, 139, 140–2*; of the valley, *95, 138*
Limonium (statice), *54,* **56, 61**
Line arrangements, *27, 34–5*
Logs, *81*
Lords and ladies, *91*

Lotus, **57, 60,** *62, 79*
Lupin, **84**

Maidenhair fern, see *Adiantum cuneatum*
Maple, *12,* **40, 71, 88**
Maranta leuconeura, 132, 152; *makoyana* (peacock plant), **119, 132,** *150*
Marguerite, *98–9*
Marigold, *59*
Mass arrangements, *27*
Mealy bug, **125,** *127–9*
Mimosa, *52*
Monkey puzzle, **72**
Monstera deliciosa (Swiss cheese plant), **151,** *152*
Moss, *14, 35, 42–3, 50,* **78**
Mother-in-law's tongue, see *Sansevieria trifasciata laurentii*
Mother of thousands, see *Saxifraga stolonifera*
Mounting, *54–5*
Mushroom, **73,** *79*

Narcissus, *19, 27, 93, 95, 97, 103, 138,* **146**
Nasturtium, *37,* **85**
Neorgelia, *152*
Nerine, *42, 142*
Nertera depressa, 152
New Zealand flax, *69*
Nicandra, **44, 57**
Nicotiana, **25**
Nidularium marechati, 152
Norfolk island pine, see *Araucaria excelsa*

Oasis, see Foamed plastic
Oats, *55, 80*
Olearia, *83, 86*
Orchid, *9, 100–2, 103,* **104,** *140–1,* **141**

Palette plant, see Anthurium
Pampas grass, see Cortaderia
Pansy, *12, 37,* **85**
Peacock plant, see *Maranta makoyana*
Pelargonium, *37, 59, 85,* **141,** *153*
Pellionia pulchra, 132, 153
Peperomia, *132,* **146, 147,** *153*
Peppers, *95, 100*
Perilla, *85*
'Period' arrangements, *12*
Perpetuelles, *53–63*
Pests, *108, 119, 123,* **125,** *126–9*
Petiole, *77*
Philodendron, *103,* **105, 113,** *114, 133, 154*
Physalis (Chinese lantern), *54, 59, 66, 73*
Piggy tail plant, see Anthurium
Pin-holders, **20, 23,** *27–9, 39, 43, 48–9,* **49,** *95, 98*

Platycerium alicorne (stag's horn fern), **153,** *154*
Plectanthrus fruticosus, 154
Poinsettia, see *Euphorbia pulcherimma*
Polyanthus, **44,** *90, 138*
Poppy, *42, 52,* **57,** *58,* **84,** *98*
Posy, *10, 14–6, 34, 66, 80, 103*
Pot-et-fleur, 13, 81, 102–6, **105**
Preserved flowers and plants, **44,** *53–63,* **57**
Primrose, *34, 80, 108*
Primula, **117**
Privet, *70,* **88,** *97*
'Profile', *22–4*
'Puddle pots', *133–4, 138–9*
Pyrethrum, *98–9*

Quaking grass, see Briza

Red spider mite, *127*
Re-potting, *123–6*
Rhodanthe, *55,* **56, 61,** *63*
Rhododendron, *79*
Rhoicissus rhomboidea (grape ivy), *114, 154*
Rhubarb, *95*
Ricinus, **96**
Ropes, *73–5, 79*
Rose, *12, 37,* **40,** *42, 59, 62, 66,* **89,** *92, 93,* **93–4,** *95, 103*
Rubber plant, see Ficus
Rush, *55–6*

S line, see 'Lazy S'
Saffron spike, see *Aphelandra squarrosa louisae*
Saintpaulia ionantha (African violet), *108, 111–112, 119, 129, 154*
Salix daphnoides, 87
Sansevieria, **112–3** and *cover*; *hahnii, 132, 154*; *trifasciata laurentii* (mother-in-law's tongue), *106, 114*
Saponaria, **44**
Saxifraga sarmentosa tricolor, 132; stolonifera (mother of thousands), *154*
Saxifrage, *86, 133*
Scabious, *99*
Scalding, *52, 98*
Scale (pest), *129*
Scindapsus aureus, 133, 154
Sea fans, *62, 98*
Seaweed, *11*
Seed heads and pods, *22,* **44,** *53,* **57,** *58, 59,* **60,** *62, 64, 66, 79, 82,* **84**
Seeds, *53, 55, 59*
Selaginella, *132*
Senecio, *83, 86*
Setsuka, *87*
Sheaf, *19*
Shells, *43, 50, 62, 95*
Shrimp plant, see *Beloperone guttata*
Silk oak, see Grevillea
Silver birch, *81*
Singeing, *52*
Siphon effect, *31, 82*
Skeletonisation, *11, 53,* **71,** *83, 95*
Snake skin plant, see *Fittonia argyroneura*
Snowdrop, *32, 108*
Snowflakes, *123–6, 131–2, 134, 140–2*
Solanum capsicastrum (winter cherry), 154
Solomon's seal, *82*
Sonerila margaritacea, 155, **155**
Spindle berries, **40**
Spring, *34, 35, 42, 83, 90, 95, 108, 137, 138, 139, 140, 142*
Spruce, *66,* **67,** *70*
Spurge, *52, 85,* **88**
Squirrel tail, *55, 91*
Stag's horn fern, see *Platycerium alicorne*
Statice, see Limonium
Starfish plant, see Cryptanthus
Stem-holders, *14–6,* **17,** *27–9, 31, 39, 43, 45–50,* **46, 51,** *81, 99, 103*; see also Foamed plastic, Pin-holders, Wire netting
Sticky buds, *32, 39*
Stipa pennata, 91
Stones, pebbles, *35, 43, 50, 62, 102–3, 133–4, 135, 138,* **146**
Strawdaisy, see Helichrysum
Summer, *34, 39, 53, 54, 58, 59,* **65,** *98, 139*
Sunflower, *59*
Swags, *48,* **71,** *73–5, 79–80*
Sweet corn, *79*
Sweet pea, *37, 38,* **65,** *87, 99*
Swiss cheese plant, see *Monstera deliciosa*
Symmetrical traditional arrangements, **15, 18,** *20–6*
Syngonium podophyllum (goose foot), *155*

Table arrangements, *10, 16, 19–20, 39, 42–3,* **61,** *62, 64, 66, 79–81,* **93,** *97, 99, 135*
Teazel, **57,** *62*
Tellima, **88**
Temperature, *51, 53, 108–11, 114–6, 136, 138–42*
Tetrastigma, *112*
Thuja, **67**
Timothy grass, *55*
Tomatoes, **85,** *100*
Tradescantia, **47,** *114, 133, 136*; *fluminensis* (wandering Jew or wandering sailor), *155*
Triangle arrangements, **25,** *26–7, 30, 35*
Tulip, *37, 77, 95, 97, 103, 114, 139* and *cover*

Verbascum, *59, 82*
Viburnum, *137*

Vinca, **116**
Volck solution, *129*

Wall decorations, *79–80*, *115*
Wallflower, *12*, *90*
Wandering Jew, wandering sailor, see *Tradescantia fluminensis*
Wax flower, see Hoya
Weddings, *21*, *64*, **65**
Wheat, *55*, *80*
Wild flowers, *12*, *53*, *55*, *80*, *91*
Willow, *87*; pussy, *87*
Winter, *34*, *35*, *39*, *53*, *58*, *64*, *79*, *83*, *86*, *137*, *138*, *140*; cherry, see *Solanum capsicastrum*
Wire, florist's, *54–5*, *68*, *70*, *74*, *75*, **75,** *76*, *79*; netting, **17,** *42*, *43*, *45–8*, **46, 47,** *49–50*, *63*, *70*, *74*, **78,** *87*, *90*

Yew, *74*

Zebra plant, see *Aphelandra squarrosa louisae*
Zebrina pendula, *156*
Zygocactus truncatus (Christmas cactus), *156*